GIFTS
from the
EDGE

GIFTS FROM THE EDGE

Lessons from the Other Side

Book : Two

© Copyright 2019 by Claudia Watts Edge

ISBN: 978-0-9994635-4-3

Library of Congress Control Number: 2019918387

Internal photographs:

Cover Photo: Denis Belitskiy, Dreamstime.com

All conceptual content and unique language are protected under this copyright. All rights reserved. No part of this publication may be reproduced or transmitted in any form or by any means electronic, mechanical, or manual, including photocopying, recording, or any information storage or retrieval system, without written permission from the author—except for brief excerpts by reviewers.

Author's Note

Many years ago, I was inspired to write a book. I was fourteen and fascinated with dying and all of the drama that surrounded it. The subject matter more interesting to me than what was being presented in school. I wanted to find the answers to seemingly unanswerable questions. I wanted to know what really happens when one leaves and goes to that unknown place.

The story was about grief and loss, and the unabated loneliness of those left behind. The main character was a dramatic older version of myself, and deeply in love with a boy she grew up with. Theirs was a promise to marry and live happily ever, but as fate would have it, his draft lottery number would come up, and serving in the Viet Nam War would have to come first. She would be forced to say goodbye to him, twice. The first as he boarded the bus heading to training camp, and the second, well you get it, he doesn't come back.

It was a love story that would survive beyond the grave, the grieving young woman would dutifully visit the cemetery every day, placing flowers on the headstone that carried his name. She began to notice the flowers she brought the day before had been rearranged, or the sealed envelopes of letters she left for him had been opened, had they been read? Was someone playing thoughtless pranks on her already raw emotions? As the clues developed, she began to wonder, perhaps he was not dead, or at least not gone forever. Did he live on? And was he aware of what was happening from the great beyond?

Pretty deep stuff for a kid who had not really experienced this kind of loss. Yes, I was quite dramatic, or at least a very deep thinker. I worked on this manuscript for hours at a time, all of it in a handwritten notebook, long before the days of the home computer. Eventually I would put it all away, as I was caught up in life's wonderful, hormonal, chaotic, teenage bliss that would create its own kind of drama.

Months later, my dad, the most kind, understanding, and handsome man a daughter could ever hope for was killed in a horrific accident at work. Many more things were put aside after that, including my need to create drama, I had plenty of it now, thanks, I guess. Be careful what you wish for.

I think back now to the book that never came to fruition, though my curiosity in the goings on after leaving this world started early and has never ceased. The death of my father was an introduction into the hard reality of loss, but also an invitation to search for real answers. I am happy to share what I have learned through many years of research into the depths of the spiritual realm through dream communication with the Other Side.

For eons, man has told stories to entertain and teach. Contained within these pages are the gifts of lessons that my dreams bring. They are sent to me in the form of a story, and I am to be its teller. Many examples and lessons are clearly marked parable or metaphor and I make sure to clearly identify them as such. I am inspired to share what has come to me from the Light, and I use very little speculation about the meaning of these dreams, because they are meant to be interpreted by you, Dear Reader, for the meaning that they will hold for you.

- Written in Love and Light
Claudia Watts Edge

Foreword

by Charol Messenger

Across the Bridge of Life

C ocooned within these treasured words and pictures of the Other Side, comfort and peace pervade me.

Gifts from the Edge: Lessons from the Other Side is an indelible contribution to all souls on Earth, and those beyond. Vivid details and recollections draw us in, so tangible that we feel like we have been there.

Claudia immediately takes us into her own dramatic near-death at age thirty-one during the tragic birth of her fifth child. We are immersed in her out-of-body journey through a tunnel in the in-between—until she returns to us with memories of and a connection with the life beyond in the light.

Now with access through the doorway, Claudia is a way show-er between the worlds. Still in vivid contact today, she gives us pictures of the Other Side, including conversations with those have who have passed. She shows us what it is like when we leave our physical body and continue to live an active life in a new healthy, young, and vibrant body. We see what it is like on the Other Side for our loved ones, and someday for ourselves, their daily lives and work. In this second *Gifts from the Edge,* the Other Side is as real a place as any other.

In *Lessons from the Other Side,* again we feel Claudia's love of all others, her open heart and selfless spirit. Reading this down-to-earth book is like a warm hug. Claudia writes with a pure heart and unvarnished honesty, weaving stories and painting pictures in a poetic style as she reveals how the next life is as tangible to those there as our lives are to us here, except without the hardships and struggles. Through her vivid details, we comprehend the scope of the expansive new life beyond our noisy, painful world. And while we still live in a world of disarray, this bigger picture gives us hope.

I met Claudia a few years ago when she came to my small house in west Denver for a personal soul reading. She glowed with poise and grace, and I was immediately engaged by her enthusiasm for her spiritual journey. She had just discovered, by chance, one of my own books *Humanity 2.0: The New Humanity* at an out-of-the-way old used bookstore off the beaten path. She had been led to it through her intuition, and my higher consciousness writing had inspired her.

I understand Claudia's writings because I also bridge the gulf and bring back insights and teachings from the spiritual realms. Prior to my own spontaneous cosmic awakening in November 1975, I too hungrily absorbed the writings of Raymond Moody, M.D. and the Seth books by Jane Roberts, among many spirituality authors. Since then, I have been writing several of my own books. This is how I can say unequivocally that Claudia Edge gifts us with unmatchable stories and insights beyond what anyone else has shared, past or present, although still reflective of the principles that I and others are receiving.

Like Claudia, after my own brush with death and dramatic awakening into a higher perspective, I no longer fear death. It is affirming to see another earthly being know the calm joy and certain contentment and clarity that come from having visited the world beyond ours and from touching the Divine presence of God and the angels, and discovering that we get to keep being that joyful, awakened person.

Relishing Claudia's sense of humor and embracing all she has seen and shares with us, washing over me and what remains with me is the majesty of truth.

- Charol Messenger
Awakened visionary, futurist, clairvoyant
Honoree of Marquis Who's Who in America 2020
Author of *In Jesus' Words, Today; Wings of Light; The Soul Path; You 2.0; Humanity 2.0: The New Humanity; The New Humans;* and *Intuition for Every Day,* among others at Amazon and Barnes and Noble.

Reviews

"Claudia Edge offers us a series of dazzling vignettes, each a precious gem in its own right, but combined, present us with a sweeping mosaic that reminds us that the Divine manifests itself in both profoundly subtle and overt ways. Edge whole-heartedly shares her spiritual journey from a deeply human perspective. Her entries are no saccharine-sweet frosting of new age platitudes, designed to spackle over the often-difficult work of transformation, but hardscrabble dispatches from the front lines of real life filled with ambiguity, uncertainty, and unspeakable beauty. "Not around, but through," psychologist Carl Jung famously reminds us and Edge shares from a place of grounded spirituality fused with sharp clarity that painful grief and an abiding belief in the afterlife are not mutually exclusive. This chronicle of wonder takes you into the day-to-day world of an everyday mystic and will inspire you to witness the small miracles that happen all around you. Indeed, these snapshots will do more than amuse and astonish, they will lead you to a place of new clarity - and most importantly, make it all but impossible to ever fear death again."

- Gregg Unterberger, M.Ed., psychotherapist and author of *The Quickening: Leaping Ahead on Your Spiritual Journey*

"An amazing compilation of stories, like a deep conversation with your best friend, drawn from dreams, thoughts, and life! Some will break your heart, some will lift your heart and some will challenge your understanding of reality. One of these stories is not like the others with a revelation so deep it will rock you. As you get to know the thoughtful caring soul of Claudia Watts Edge through her stories, you get the opportunity to love her!"

   - Mary Deioma, Author of *Loved: A Transcendent Journey* and *Seven Steps for Enlightenment, Practical Steps Anyone Can Take Toward Personal Enlightenment.* Founder of Sun Whisperers.

"Claudia's beautiful book is the summary of one major life lesson learnt during her charming encounters with the enchanting spiritual realms above, and that is love and Kindness. Her powerful testimony emerges from depths of despair to immense brilliance of Love/Light that guides her heart and all that ever exists in creation. No-wonder it can be an enlightening balm for hearts brutalized by deepest sorrow of losing a loved one on earth. It's difficult to imagine how a young woman in her teens would have dealt with the pain of losing two of her pillars and mighty pillars which held her life. Yet, indeed as she succinctly expresses that all that matters is the goodness in one's heart. Her powerful testimony is a unique summary of the fact that it was the goodness in her heart which led her to heavenly encounters and in her charming writings brought forth a soothing balm for readers. Her mesmerizing writing springs forth from a deeper understanding of the mysteries of universe and life. There are many books that describe the spiritual realms but Claudia's unique near-death experience reveals very practically the hard truths regarding earth and heavens. The most charming aspect of her experience is the reader develops immense faith in the spirit worlds and the Divinity that governs all existence. Thanks Claudia for sharing your wonderful spiritual gifts and lessons."

   - Dr Rohit Gour, Asst Professor *Jazan University Saudi Arabia.*

"This brilliant, daring, and gifted author has blessed all who will be reading her latest book! I read it in two days as I was having trouble putting it down to take care of my activities of daily living. We are encouraged and reminded to TRUST all of it. I loved this book!"

   - Becki Hawkins, Speaker and Author of *Transitions: A Nurse's Education About Life and Death.*

"Claudia Edge has generously shared more of her Gifts from the Edge with the world, and the world is richer for of it. Some of us have been gifted with experiences of undeniable magic, and in her second book,

Edge shows us again that she has been privileged to witness some of the most spectacular ever recorded. I am dazzled by her accounts, and at the same time overwhelmed by the warmth of her extraordinary heart. Her words will make you feel like she is your treasured sister, mother, friend, or grandmother. Her accounts are a delightful blending of human vulnerability and the supernatural, and reading them will make you realize that you too, no matter how ordinary your life may seem, are open to receiving gifts like these, far beyond our understanding."

- John Melody MS, Editor

Contents

Author's Note i

Foreword by Charol Messenger iii
   Across the Bridge of Life iii

Reviews vi

The Art of Death and Dying 1
   The ten things that dying taught me 1
   Into the Darkness 6
   The Smoky Essence 17
   I Died Last Year 18
   The Great Dash 19
   What Dying Looks Like 21
   The Warm Glimpse 24

After-Life Communication 27
   A Slow Start 27
   The Number 432 31
   Just a Phone Call Away 33
   Artistic Impressions 36
   Talladega Nights and Other Gatherings 38
   Not the Strong Stuff 39
   Blocking Grief 42
   The Missing State of Delaware 46
   Coincidental Message 47

The Importance of Dreams 49
   A Very Personal Effect 51
   The Boy I Knew 53
   Another Dream Scenario 55
   The Dream 55
   This is All We Will Speak of That 57

    Of Black Elk and Dreams 58
    Peeling Energy 60
    Expecting to Fly 63

The Astral Plane 65
    What Is the Astral Plane? 65
    Lucy 67
    The Special Bus 68
    Double Pane 70

The Seeker 73
    Soul to Soul 74
    For the Briefest of Moments 75
    Hey, Has Anyone Got a Key? 76
    Wow… Did I Get Read 77
    An Old Friend Drops In 78
    I Would Love Them 81
    The Universal Outreach 82
    Truman's World 84

Who Are you, Really? 87
    A Very Special Visit 87
    Walk with Me 90
    Inadequate 92
    Ego and Self-Esteem Spirit School 94
    Hello, Soldier 96
    Becoming a Bridge,
    Its Importance and Responsibility 96
    The Act of Balance 98
    The Valves Are Us 99

Do Not Let Fear Become Your Story 103
    Letting Go of Fear 103
    Right Turns Only 107
    Solo 108
    Squishing Arachnophobia 110

Reincarnation, The Big Picture 115
    A Visual of Our Many Lives 117

A 360-Degree View 118
Nudges and Flashpoints 119
We Are Not Set Up to Fail or Fall 120
The Big Life Exam 121
The Theatre of Life is a Gift 122
Earth-Life Theatre 122
My Other Lives 123
The Wheel of Lives 132
Choosing a Body 134
Trying Out a Life 136
Sister/Friend 138
Lots of Me's 141

Pause and Reflect 147
Life's Ride is Full of Carnival Balloons 147
Grandma, Are You Not Brave? 149
Dance with Me 151
Moon Walks with Jude 153
Deep-Diving Angel 154
Did You Realize
We Have Been Talking for 11 Minutes? 159
My Resolve 162
Jeff's Star 163
The Heavens do not Disappoint! 164

A Change Is Gonna Come 167
The Twelve Apostles 167
Mastodons and Flying Machines 170
New Earth Second Earth 171
Black Crystal Healing Chambers 172
The Place of Universal Knowledge 174
Some Things Are Set 176
Paper Mache 177
The Big Wave 178
Looking into the Crater 179

Soft Speak 183
She Just Needed to Be Heard 183

  A Stranger Connection 186
  The Tree of Death and Life 188
  What a Difference
  a Few Kind Words Can Make 190
  The Woman in the Babushka 192

Life's Success Before Dying 195
  Re-Friended 195
  Karma Gettcha 198
  The Cancer Holidays 200
  Halt, Who Goes There, Friend or Foe? 202
  The Water Story 203

Aging is a Beautiful Process 207
  Letting Go of Needless Things 207
  Authenticity and Wrinkled Skin 208
  Tick Tock 209

The Children Are Our Future 211
  Perfect Days 212
  Grandma, I Have
  Some Good News and Some Bad News 214
  Some Special Attention 216
  Accentuate the Positive 217

Epilogue 219
  Small Bites 219
  For My Forever Sister 221
  Dear Mom 221

Thank You 224

About the Author 226

GIFTS
from the
EDGE

Lessons from the Other Side

Book II

CLAUDIA WATTS EDGE

"The important thing is not to stop questioning. Curiosity has its own reason for existence. One cannot help but be in awe when he contemplates the mysteries of eternity, of life, of the marvelous structure of reality. It is enough if one tries merely to comprehend a little of this mystery each day."

- Albert Einstein

1

The Art of Death and Dying

The ten things that dying taught me

I died in 1984, years before it was commonplace to hear about the NDE (near-death experience). The survivors' stories are showing up all over now in movies and books. Even the television news is adding to the growing curiosity and to societies' quiet acceptance since the early years of this phenomenon. It is hard to imagine that one can actually die and be brought back to life, and each experience has quite a story to tell, and the telling of the story also comes with a deep sense of responsibility.

Most people are not as interested in how death happened, but in what happened while in the great beyond. What was seen and what was heard? The articles and books are scanned for the meat of the story, and the beautiful descriptions and feelings of what it was like to be in heaven. Each death story is unique and different for each individual, and yet there is much common ground in the life-after-life story.

*Following is a synopsis
of what I was allowed to bring back with me.*

1 – Dying is easy. You've done it many times before.

As John Lennon said, "I'm not afraid of death because I don't believe in it. It's just getting out of one car and into another." To spend your life fearing the inevitable would be a wasted life. Do your best with every day knowing that some days are going to feel better than others. Lay your head down at night assured that you have done your best with the hours within it. Did you do your best? Because that is a measure of a good day, and no matter how small your achievements may appear to someone else, when you are satisfied within yourself, you have nothing to fear when your time comes.

2 – You are here for a reason.

This life is not an accidental happenstance. But rather, a carefully coordinated play that you and others around you contracted to participate in for the experience and advancement of spiritual growth. Think of it as the Holodeck of Star Trek fame, it is very real as you participate, and after exiting, you get to examine the experience and learn from it. Our lives are a marvel of complicated orchestration, and a gift of love from the Creator. It is carefully set up to bring a desired outcome, and before you were born you worked with your higher counsel and the souls around you to assist in bringing it all into fruition. The goal is to achieve the highest outcome, but the plan is not set in stone, and can be adapted as 'Free Will Choices' are made while here. Our Free Will trumps all pre-planning and contractual agreements.

3 – You are not alone.

You have many who cheer you on from the Other Side, guides, angels, passed loved ones and ancestors have your back as they nudge you towards your intended goal. You have helped yourself with pre-determined road signs and red flags set to nudge you along the way.

You were also born with the gift of intuition, it is within you to know and feel when something is off, or not quite right, and if you will stop and listen, it can be of great assistance.

The veil of forgetfulness was necessary, as we must leave the perfection of our connectedness behind, in order to play the game of 'life.' The separation and loneliness that you feel while here is intended and is necessary, and not a shunning from God.

4 – We are part of the whole.

We are magnificent souls, each an individual thread of Source, our Creator. We, all of us, are necessary to be a complete whole and unified piece, and we are all valued and loved equally as we bring our physical experiences back to share with the spiritual realm. This can only be accomplished by our working together, as none of us will be left behind. All are necessary and needed to weave the perfect tapestry of God.

5 – The universe is teaming with life, and the stars are alive and conscious.

While in the rapidly moving tunnel, I found myself in deep space. The tunnel was like a bubble that I could see through, and it provided a perfect vantage point to see and hear the stars as I zoomed past them. Upon approach, the colors would stretch out as if they were moving with me with bright yellow as the main color, followed with patches of red, pink and blue as if they were being licked by fire. The movement created a tail, like a current or a wave, which is where most of the color changes took place. The stars have their own voices, and they grew louder the closer I got. They spoke to me as welcoming and joyful friends, all seeming to have an intimate knowledge of me.

We have many brothers and sisters who are on their own journeys of discovery on many different planets within the universe. Each location is purposeful in its creation for what it offers toward further knowledge, learning abilities and spiritual development.

6 – Earth is one of the lowest, hardest places to experience.

Congratulations and bravo, you are both brave and magnificent to have chosen this path of rapid advancement. Achievements here are expedited, which is the attraction of choosing Earth, but they are also extremely hard fought as the struggle for survival is pitted with starvation, hatred, emotional scarring, illness and physical maladies imposed while here. Believe me, you are a rock star and much admired for your bravery.

7 – There is a place in Heaven to recuperate.

It is a type of hospital, a respite from the journey here, many stay in a recuperative state for a while after their mission is complete. The esoteric (spiritual) body may be in need of repair from the journey here, worn down with illness and the like, and the soul may also need more time to be re-introduced into the spirit realm. I was shown that my own mother needed this extra time of convalescing, as her entire earthly life was spent expecting a certain outcome from years of religious conditioning. It was shocking and confusing to her to find an entirely different construct in the afterlife than what she had been taught.

8 – Believe it or not, you will want to come back again.

This is the reincarnation that we hear about. What I was shown is that coming back is necessary to complete lessons. It is a 360-degree opportunity to walk in another's shoes, and to learn from all sides of the equation. If you are a thief, you will experience loss as a victim next time, but not as a karmic punishment, but from a different viewpoint for a complete understanding. Can anything good come from the grief of losing a loved one? And can anything good come from such pain? Yes, and it is a planned opportunity, as awful as that sounds here in human form, but yes, much good comes from your pain and suffering. A patient racked with illness leads to an opportunity for others to serve. There can be no more of a complete lesson, than what is experienced from all sides.

You will be excited to do it again because the experience is everything. What is brought back to be shared is the goal. The sacrifice of a 'short' amount of time to achieve the intended goal is inconsequential compared to the lesson it will provide for yourself, and the others who will absorb and incorporate it, including God/Source. We are the tools that God uses to experience the physical. We are important foot soldiers in the continued development of God's Unconditional Love and Knowledge.

9 – You are worthy of God's love and do not need a middleman to have a relationship with God.

I wish it were possible to convey the love that I was shown by God in my experience. I was allowed to know how he truly felt about me through his eyes. It is hard to explain, but I was pulled outside of the scene, and was soon watching myself as God saw me. I was overwhelmed at the pride I had in my own self, even saying aloud, "Wow, she is doing so good, isn't she?" I do not mean to come off as prideful here, but there will be no higher compliment or achievement for me than to have witnessed his love for me. I am happy to know that one day you will all feel it again too, because you are Magnificent in his eyes, and HE LOVES YOU, UNCONDITIONALLY!

10 – Your life review is not intended as a punishment or judgment.

Love and knowledge mean everything, it is all we get to bring back with us, and it is the star of our life review. There is no punishment or sentence put on us, there is only the opportunity to learn from a perceived mistake. Once you have completed your mission, it is reviewed by a counsel of trusted individuals who love you and have only your best interest at heart. Cause and effects of our choices are revealed as grateful lessons. We will watch ourselves in various scenes of our lives, and we will see and feel our actions towards others and how it affected them by actually 'feeling' their reactions to what we said, and what we did. Seemingly simple occurrences, such as a forgotten bus stop when we shared a smile or conversed with a stranger that may have saved a life, and you would never know it until you see the ripples of your actions during your review.

After seeing mine, I knew the feeling of pride in the ripples of positive action that stemmed from a simple kindness. I also felt the sting of an action that was careless and thoughtless, and the sting is memorable. Your review is not judgement, and no one there has an intent of punishment, you will be much harder on yourself than any of your guides and counsel. Their job is to let you see your own actions so you can learn from them in a setting of love and acceptance. And that dear reader is the purpose of our Journey.

Into the Darkness

My Earth-Death Experience

It has taken me thirty-five years to tell this story, but the time is finally right for me to open up and share it.

At the age of thirty-one, I was in a full-term pregnancy with my fifth child. Having birthed four healthy babies, I was confident of a safe outcome this time. It had been suggested that with such a good health history, I could save a lot of money and inconvenience to my family if I worked with a midwife for this birth. For some reason though, I never took the advice seriously, and was now only a day away from my due date when my uterus clamped down into a very hard contraction at home.

At first, I was excited, knowing that I would soon meet the little person I carried, but after several hours of this non-stop contraction of my uterus, I began to feel very uncomfortable.

The contraction was stuck, it was intense and strong and the result was my uterus was as hard as a rock. The baby's foot felt like it had been caught in my rib cage, and I was worried about how he/she was doing overall, so I decided it was time to head for the hospital.

The admitting nurse was torn, because technically, I had only had one contraction. But because this was to be my fifth baby, she decided to keep me close with orders to walk the halls of the hospital to help things along. It was going to be a long night, and the doctor was told to roll over and go back to sleep, and they would contact him when there was more to report.

I did as I was asked, setting off down the hallway to explore the hospital, but only got as far as the elevator doors. Not much of a walk really, and by the time the doors slid open I was too out of breath to board, and promptly sat down in a wheelchair parked nearby. I told my husband that I just didn't feel right, and that I wanted to go back. At first, he was confused, why did I want to return to the pre-natal floor after being sent away only minutes before, but I was following my instinct. I'm going to emphasize this by repeating, I FOLLOWED MY INSTINCT one of the many I would have during the upcoming events, and I headed back to the exam room.

The nurse was surprised to see me back so soon. But I told her that I just didn't feel right, and so she obliged and began admitting procedures, sending my husband out to the waiting room with a clip board full of insurance questions.

I was sent to the dressing room with a traditional open backed hospital gown, and while undressing I noticed a drop of blood on the floor, followed shortly by another, and soon realized the blood was coming from me. I promptly pushed the red button for the nurse's assistance. There was a concerned tone in my voice as I explained that this had never happened to me before, and the nurse tried to tell me this was all perfectly normal, and that I had probably just pushed too hard when going to the bathroom. I began to disagree, that no, I had not yet been to the bathroom, but before I could finish my protest, all hell broke loose.

It was as if there was a bucket between my legs filled with blood, and it had tipped over, spilling its contents all over the floor. The nurse's shoes were covered in it, and it's warmth at my feet faded as soon as it hit the cold floor, and a distinct metallic smell wafted through the air.

Bucket after bucketful spilled out, as the nurse's face was bathed with an astonished gasp as she pushed me onto a nearby gurney. She began to yell orders, telling me to lay down at the same time she began to yell for help. An emergency was called out, CODE BLUE CODE BLUE and a call for a doctor to come to the exam room immediately. There was no time to go anywhere else. I was in big trouble and we all knew it.

Out of a helpless concern for my unborn child, a noise began to climb out of my throat. A combination of shock and fear formed an instinctive low-pitched cry for survival. This guttural moan rose from resources deep within me, creating a sound so primal, I even scared myself.

My doctor had been called, but there was no time to wait for him, still some 30 minutes out, and soon a shiny new intern entered the room. He was being gowned in front of me, and I noticed that he was looking at an instruction book until they slapped gloves on him.

I kept thinking about the fact that I had no pain and yet I was dying. I knew this because I was told so, not intentionally, but in crisis, the staff needs to instruct each other, and patient sensitivity, is pretty much thrown out the window. I do not say this in a derogatory way, as I was grateful I could listen in and try to grasp what was happening to me. The doctor assessed the scene and proclaimed that I had two minutes of blood left, so I figured that this was going to be it for me, and I kind of relaxed into a resolve as I thought, so this is how it ends, Wow.

The nurse kept pulling a sheet up over my face, I'm sure she was only trying to shield me from the gruesome sight, but I wasn't dead yet, and I was in no mood to look or act like I was.

There was so much blood on the floor everyone was slipping about, their shoes acting more like ice skates. They clung to the gurney for fear of slipping and falling into the red pool below. In any other context the scene would have been really funny.

A cleaning woman came into the room, holding a thick mop, and dragging a large metal pail behind her. She was trying to clear an area on the floor for the doctor to work, she swabbed the deck as best she could, as I continued to spill out life giving fluid.

A surgical tray was brought in, and a light was adjusted over me, it was all going to go down right here. I continued to pull at the sheet covering my face, this job becoming harder now, as a team began to assemble along the side of the table where I lay. Each one held down an arm or leg, there was no time for straps or proper blankets, or anesthesia for that matter, oh yeah, did I mention that there was no doctor of anesthesia available, so this surgery was going to be done 'pioneer style.'

A nurse said that she could no longer get a reading of the baby's heartbeat, Oh God, please hurry! I thought, and the doctor's part of the show began. He pulled at my gown and exposed my full belly, and then picked up the scalpel, and I saw it flash under the light. The nurse noticed the fear on my face, and she gave him a quick shoulder tap as she nodded in my direction, and he understood what she was trying to convey. I was still very much awake and alive, and I was watching everything, and he took in a deep breath before he looked me directly in the eye for the first time since his arrival, and said, "I have to do this" and I shook my head in agreement, "yes, please save my baby."

I could feel the long slow cut as the doctor slid the sharp instrument along my exposed skin. My thought was that it hadn't hurt that much because as a kid I had some wild idea that putting salt in my cuts would help them heal faster, and so this kind of pain was familiar in that way. This is only stinging, I told myself, like salt in a wound, and I was glad to have developed a high tolerance to pain, good for me I thought. I can take it, I'll be OK.

I watched everything going on around me, taking note of what was being said and done, until I began to notice a change in the room. The ceiling began to lift away and it disappeared as the walls became fluid and wavelike, and they began to move inward toward me. I thought that the light in the room was growing dimmer, and I blinked several times to make sure. Yes, in spite of the direct lighting, it was getting dark, and I began to feel a slight tugging from behind.

I tried to focus on my heart, laying as still as possible, trying to slow down every precious beat as it pumped out my life's blood. The doctor was through the skin now, a giant vertical cut through the middle of my belly, stem to stern, not great for bikini wearing, but it created a good emergency exit for my baby. I was handling the pain, and noted, that I was still OK.

The room grew darker still, and the walls began to form a tunnel all around me, I tried to focus on what the doctor was doing, anxious for my child to come into the world, UNTIL .... OH GOD, THE PAIN!

A nurse stood near my feet, holding an armful of long grey rope, and I soon realized this grey rope was my intestines. There was nowhere to climb away from the pain this action caused, though my legs were certainly trying.

Even my ears screamed, this kind of pain is unimaginable, and I struggle to find the words to explain the intensity of it. A soldier on the battlefield with a gut wound that promises certain death, this kind of pain was now mine, and my mind screamed, FAINT DAMN IT! CLAUDIA, FAINT! Why could I not make myself swoon like a southern belle! I wanted out! Please faint now!

But I did not faint, instead I struggled against those who held down my arms and legs as I tried to roll away from the fear and agony. More helpers came in to hold me down, including the woman holding the mop, all trying to keep me still, as all of my inner workings were being displaced.

The only part of me that was able to move were my fingers and sadly the only thing they found to cling to for comfort was the soft under hanging skin of the cleaning woman's arm. She was older and plump and I was aware enough to see her knee's buckle as I grabbed hold and held fast. I can remember mouthing the words "I'm so sorry" towards her, the words seemed to come out in slow motion, but her face was grimaced too tightly to notice. I knew she was suffering, but I could not let go, I was clamped on and shut down for the long haul of it, and she and her poor arms under hangings were along for the ride.

The walls continued to close in and soon I was almost completely engulfed within them.

So, this is the tunnel I had heard about, everything closes inward from both the front, and the sides, creating a tunnel, and I was slowly being pulled backward as it formed.

I could hardly see anything now, but as I lost one sense, the others amplified in strength. My hearing became acute, this sense was super charged, and I could hear everything within the entire hospital, machine's beeping noises, people talking, and phones ringing, I could hear it all.

I heard the doctor say the baby had drowned. The blood that fed and warmed her as she grew, had now brought a horrible end, and I could not take much more. My anguish at the loss of my baby was more intense than the physical pain.

I focused on some music, hearing it as easily as if it was being played on a loudspeaker. It was the theme song from the television show 'Mash' the 'Suicide is Painless' song....and I knew it had to be 10:35 because Mash always followed the 10 o'clock news. Realizing it was 10:35 in the midst of all that was going on all around me was crazy, but I noted the fact that my baby had died, and now I was dying while I listened to music, and it was 10:35 in the evening.

The faint tugging at me had now turned into a pulling feeling, and as I moved backwards into the darkened tunnel the walls had made, I popped out of my body. It was easy, a soft pop, like the air in a child's pop gun toy, pop and out. It felt perfectly normal to leave my body on the table behind me, the scene was gruesome and I no longer wanted to look at it, and I became more interested in finding out where the music was coming from.

I found myself floating into the adjacent waiting room, and I could see my husband sitting with his head down as he worked on the insurance forms. I felt bad that he had no idea what was going on behind the closed doors, and that my family would soon learn of our fate. This was going to be hard on them all, but it was also more than I could conceive of at the time, and so I continued on my way across the ceiling. I was busy figuring out this new floating thing, and soon found myself in the open hallway.

I paused next to the clock that hung out from the wall, and really focused on it, yup I was right, it was 10:35. I remember noticing the sticky dust on the very top of it where no one else could possibly see, you know the dust that sticks to the top of the kitchen cabinets no matter how much you try to clean them. I thought that this clock must have been there for a long time to have so much sticky residue attached to it. Strange thoughts, I know, but the fact that I was floating above everyone else was not lost on me, it was kind of fun.

I continued on my way, my focus back on the music, and I found its source in a patient's room, an older man, sound asleep, his television left on. I hung out there for a few moments, finally realizing that he had no idea that I was there beside him, and I began to focus on what had happened to me, and this new ability to float. I realized that I had died, but that I was not dead. What I was now was very much still me, and as I considered this, everything changed, and I found myself somewhere else.

I was now in an expanse of nothingness, and in complete darkness, the kind of darkness where you can't see your hand in front of your own face. It was thick, yet fluid like, and it reminded me of the commercials showing a chocolatier pouring melted chocolate out of the pan, exposing its smooth, velvety richness. This is the closest I can come to an explanation of the darkness.

It had substance, it was alive, but I was not afraid, it was a loving presence that held me, and cradled me like a child. I was in the most comforting place of nothingness, where all thought and worries are erased. I WAS, that was it, I WAS, and that was enough. I had no reason to want anything more than this, and I stayed within the comfort of the darkness for what could have been an eternity. There were no time constraints there, although in Earth time my death would be measured in minutes.

I had died, but the blood transfusions and the promising young doctor continued, and an earthly miracle brought me from the silence, and the morgue grey color of physical death. I felt the tugging again. "NO! I am so happy here, no…. please, no, don't make me go back." There is total bliss in the expanse, and I could have stayed there forever.

The tugging turned into a strong pull, and soon I was back in my body. The most extraordinary part of my re-entry was sound. The years of adjusting and desensitizing to noisy Earth was gone, the filter had been wiped clean while in the void, and now just hearing a human voice seemed invasive to me.

Claudia… Claudia…come back now…wake up, I could hear the nurse calling out to me, the sound created an intrusive ripple of noise, eroding my blissful calm, and I had no interest in opening my eyes, I wanted to go back to the quiet of the darkness, and I kept my eyes closed in protest.

The relentless calling of my name was so irritating that I finally answered just to make it stop. I told her that my baby was dead, and that I didn't want to wake up. It took a lot of coaxing and a polaroid picture of my baby in the nursery to convince me to open my eyes and see for myself that my beautiful baby girl had been brought back to life, and that she needed me.

Her life was being measured in minutes, if she made it an hour, then three, and through the night etc. Each milestone raised the likelihood of her 'making it.' Her entry into the world had been rough, and now she would fight for every breath and endure hourly blood draws from the bottoms of her tiny feet until they were completely raw. There was a question of how long had she been 'down,' and so a bigger question loomed, had she suffered any brain damage? This was a 'wait and see' answer.

I was told that my placenta had exploded, turning living tissue into shrapnel. I'm not completely sure if it was caused by the constant contraction I had suffered earlier in the day, but it had filled up with blood until it could not hold or endure any more.

I was also told that it was a good thing that I had stayed close by, and that I would have certainly perished had I been en route, or even on the far side of the hospital for that matter. The thought of being at home with a midwife in this situation still terrifies me. I had followed my instincts, and I am grateful that the stars had aligned to create the best outcome for my family.

The full explanation of the hows and whys of it all was woven in between pharmaceutical loopiness and sleep, but I did learn that I was in for a long, hard recovery and an eventual need for a full hysterectomy.

As I recovered, vital replacement blood was supplied by wonderful volunteers. Each bag was a welcomed sight, and as the new blood entered my veins, a completely opposite effect of what I had experienced while dying took hold. The room would become brighter and more vibrant, and the walls were moving back into their proper place. It really is life's blood, and I became a thirsty vampire in the need and wanting of it.

The hospital staff had dubbed me 'pioneer woman,' and I had quite a few visitors. Some were from the original team, including the intern who now had quite a story to tell his peers.

There were questions about what it felt like going through an emergency C Section surgery without any anesthesia. The questions were understandably out of curiosity, but were also teaching/learning questions, and they were the easy ones to answer.

The question that gave me pause, was the BIG question of 'who, what, or even if' I had seen anything during my death. The long pause, coupled by an inability to form an answer, was usually taken as residual shock or trauma of the incident. After a few awkward moments, the asker would usually just excuse themselves. My silence was not meant as a refusal to answer the question, but I was having trouble formulating my own understanding of an experience that challenged my entire belief system.

I had died and come back; this I knew with absolute certainty. But my reality did not match any of the NDE experiences I had read about in Dr. Moody's, or the similar books I'd read after the tragic loss of my father many years before. His death had ignited a curiosity within me, and I needed to know where the entirety of his energy had gone. His personality had always been larger than life, and I needed to know what he was doing now that he was gone from me.

I found comfort in the stories of others who followed a bright light or heard the songs of angels and met relatives in the greenest of gardens. Why had I not seen my Father during my death experience, the man that I missed and loved so very much? I had found only darkness, and a shame began to creep inside of me, and I shut down and began to push the experience away.

I didn't want to talk about it with anyone, fearing that my time in the darkness might construe a negative judgment against me. In a religious context, darkness is evil, and negative. This is what I had been raised in church to understand. Yet, in my heart, I knew that any earthly wrongs I had committed just did not seem worthy of eternal damnation.

I knew I had not been to Hell, because where I had gone was nothing like the horror stories I had heard in Sunday School. But I was having a hard time understanding or expressing the beauty of the dark nothingness without thinking that I sounded crazy. The wonderful experience in the darkness was in complete opposition of my faith, and what I thought I knew.

The questions eventually stopped, and I was able to put my experience aside, where it stayed for over thirty years. I continued to read everything I could find on NDEs, but I never found a similar account or someone struggling over it the way I was, and I was embarrassed that I didn't have a beautiful story to share with the world.

I made it a point to meet the wonderful authors of books that filled my soul, though I had a jealous yearning for the rest of my own story. I began to ask God if darkness was to be all I would know of Heaven. Or were my instincts correct and had more taken place that had been veiled from my memory?

These questions opened the floodgates of answers. For over ten years now, I wake recalling vivid and lucid dreams, and distinct memories. My physic abilities continue to grow, and there are times that I can hear and communicate with my mother and sister who have passed.

I have given myself a gift of no longer feeling fear to say these things out loud, nor do I worry what someone else may think of me as I tell my truths. This was a big step in my spiritual development and it came in as a daytime visual, the word on a large billboard, planted in the middle of nowhere. The large black lettering sat on a pure white background that simply said, TRUST.

I have been able to let go of all the fears that I had held and was a prisoner to, and I am learning to live within the word that I keep on my desk on a simple post-it-note written in magic marker: **TRUST**

The Teaching Lessons I receive are from a loving guide I call Click Click, a different kind of name I know, but for a myriad of reasons it fits him, and he thinks it's funny.

There are mornings that I remember visiting a place I lovingly call Spirit School. It is where true higher learning takes place, sometimes set in a classroom, and sometimes out in nature. I am with other students, though I never see them that I can remember, but I know that they are there just the same. Together we learn from the most patient of teachers who work to bring us to a deeper understanding of the vast Spiritual puzzle.

These Gifts I am obligated to share.

My NDE served a purpose, and for whatever reason in my soul's progression, a deep and wonderful experience took place, I had a beautiful healthy baby girl who healed with no residual damage. She is perfect. And I survived with time to ponder and grow in my own strengths, and at a pace I was ready to handle.

The stories I write are of my journey of spiritual awakening and growth, and what I learned on the Other Side while my body lay still. These memories still continue to rise into my consciousness. I am told there is reason for the veil that blocked my experience from me, and the resulting delay of the memories of what I learned of the afterlife during my Earth death.

My curiosity had been a gift to keep me interested, and yet never quite satisfying my thirst for knowledge. This curiosity would push me to continue to explore beyond my death experience, and all nature of spiritual phenomena. I continue to receive measured samples of spiritual answers, with a need to honor an obligation to share the lessons.

The Smoky Essence

Early in my spiritual development I had a very disturbing dream. I was lucid and awake within the dream, and so I trusted the lesson being given to me because it offered a headline 'pay attention.' It begins with a flash of light = a flash of insight.

I was looking at myself in a simple everyday pose, but I was outside of me. I was looking at a uniquely 360-degree view of myself, impossible to be able to see before without the assistance of the dream.

I saw a wispy, smoky energy that began wafting out of the top of my head. I knew that it was the essence of me, and who I truly am. It had a silvery/white color to it, like clean smoke, and as it floated out of me, I saw that it had a life of its own, and it began to dance around the air where I stood. As it left, I saw that there was now an empty hollowness to the body, my body, and I was able to enter it from the top of my head. I could now see my body up close from the inside.

Yes, it was empty, the me had left, and now the body, without this lively smoky essence residing within it began to darken. The lovely pink and healthy body was now turning dark from the inside out. Within moments it was completely black and had begun to wither and shrink like a flower without life giving water.

At first this dream disturbed me, the visual was so very real, but as I lay in the dark recalling what I had seen, I soon realized that I had been gifted a chance to know what really happens to you when you die. I now have more than just a belief or faith that we go on, because I had witnessed a very real lesson.

I knew without a doubt that I WOULD STILL BE ME WITHOUT MY BODY. We will all be OK and move on as ourselves when we leave the withering physical shell of ourselves behind, and release the essence of who we truly are into the air to freely dance.

I Died Last Year

For Basia

Tis the season of going through the address book and sending holiday cards containing our Happy New Year wishes to those we care for. As I perused the alphabetized list of friends and relations, a name stood out, and I decided it was time for an overdue chat.

After a brief synopsis of how we had spent the last few years apart, she announced, "guess what, I died last year" and our conversation took a sharp turn into the spiritual phenomenon of life-after-life.

She explained that after putting a pan on the stove, she lay down for a few moments while waiting for it to boil. Exhaustion and heavy sleep took over, and soon the pan and the house around it began to burn, and its toxic smoke overtook her.

She found herself in a valley, walking down a road toward a distant horizon.

All around her, ripples and waves rose from the road, but not of heat as you would assume, but she knew with an absolute certainty that it was LOVE that was rising and wafting in front of her, and with each step, she was filled with more LOVE and PEACE than she had ever known.

Her anxious mind, usually filled with earthly worries, was calm and she felt no need to turn around and check on the busy life she was leaving behind. Her only motivation was to move forward and to bask in the LOVE that surrounded and filled her.

Meanwhile a frantic husband dragged a lifeless body outside and worked fervently to save her. After many attempts to revive her, she eventually heard her daughter's voice calling out to her, "Mom, Mom!" though her daughter was living hundreds of miles away at the time.

By the grace of God, the gallant efforts of her husband, and the sound of her daughter's voice, she was pulled back into the pain and the needs of the body. She added a sidebar that she was pretty grumpy about being brought back, wanting to stay in pursuit of the distant horizon and all that it held for her.

She said, "Claudia, I used to be scared of dying, but not anymore, I want to live the best life I can, but now I know that something wonderful awaits me, and someday, I will walk until I reach it." Needless to say, I am glad I made that long overdue call and reconnection, and that my friend was able to come back to her family and share her beautiful story.

The Great Dash

It is surprising how people can just show up in your life at the perfect time, seemingly by happenstance, though I have come to believe there are no such things as accidents.

I was supposed to meet Suzan, and practically tripped over her during a mountainside concert just outside of Denver.

She is a very loving and mothering type, and intuition told her that I could use a friend, and she was right. I was going through a rough patch in my marriage, and she literally scooped me up and pulled me into her group on that muddy hillside. I needed a shoulder, but more importantly I needed to learn what she had to teach me.

Her inner calm came from worldly experience, and she had a strong connection to the other side. She recognized coincidence and synchronicity as heavenly intervention, and I was at the point in my life that I was ready to listen and learn. I thank her to this day for her gentle nudges toward the road I now travel.

She would often tell me that she had no fear of dying, and that she felt herself in a good place with God, and so when she relayed her story aboard an airplane in trouble, I listened in fascination.

Turbulent weather over the Rockies took hold of the plane she was on, spilling luggage and people in the aisles. Many were hurt, including Suzan, a sharp snap of her head resulted in broken teeth.

I asked her about the people in the seats around her, expecting a story of heroism and the use of her innate abilities to calm terrified passengers. She laughed out loud at this and said, "Well you'd think so, but as the plane dipped and tumbled, I was screaming at the top of my lungs just like everybody else."

The timing of our deaths is left to uncertainty, though it is an inevitable fact of life that our day will come. There is a wonderful quote about living the dash, the line between the notable life dates of birth and death. The dash being the most important line of your life, as it depicts what you did with the time in-between those two dates. A good reminder to live fully, and to experience and enjoy the time granted in-between.

After the connections I made through my first book, and my years of NDE research, I continually hear from people who live stymied and afraid. Their future death seems to loom larger than their lives, letting anxiety control them, and leech into their sleep. Fear becomes their story, and it is a cancer that inhibits the ability to take chances and really live, or to ride the ride so to speak.

I write now in hopes of alleviating those fears. Dying is easy, and from my own death experience, I remember the wonder and curiosity of it, but fear was never attached to it.

I noticed a different feeling in the air, as the sounds and visuals changed around me, and I felt a soft puff, like a child's pop gun as I left my body, but it didn't hurt. The soul instinctively leaves before feeling the needless pain and suffering that is not vital to the experience.

I am not speaking of the pain of a lingering illness, or the aftermath of an unfortunate accident. This is an entirely different scenario, an intended or contracted experience agreed to long before our coming to earth. It is an opportunity for accelerated learning and experience for either the person who is ill, or their family or caretakers in offering their service.

When the mission is complete, it is time to go home, and when the soul is ready, it exits simply and easily, with an instantaneous pop, accompanied by the sound of soft wind chimes, and the ability to float. The body is left behind, the living overalls shed, and all is perfectly natural to move on without it. There is nothing to fear in the act of dying, you have done it before on many other occasions, and you will recognize that it rings of familiarity as it is happening, ahh yes, you are going home.

There should be no fear in the act of living either. God knows you, and he knows your heart and loves you unconditionally, you have gone through a lot while here, and you have done what you set out to do, finished now, you get to go home to open arms.

After years of hospice work I have learned, that how we, or a loved one faces our demise is very personal and shouldn't be judged by the grace of the exit.

Suzan's story taught me a great lesson, because she is cognizant and aware and works toward living her best life every day. She accepts the responsibility of being charitable, offering love and acceptance to others in need. Through the humor of her story aboard the ill-fated plane, she also taught me that it's OK when your time does come, that if you need to, feel free to scream your bloody head off.

What Dying Looks Like

As a hospice volunteer, I have watched many patients face the transcendental journey towards the inevitable. By the time I was to meet them, they had already battled the stages of grief and anger as they fought the formidable foe. Now the strength of the will had been replaced with acceptance and resignation.

Medical treatments are no longer a focus, and now only the last steps of care and comfort are left. The body's need for nourishment is alleviated, as the pleasure of taste has been altered to a metallic mouthful. Favorite treats brought by well-intentioned visitors are left untouched.

The only cure that can be offered is keeping the level of pain in check. Mind numbing doses of a liquid eraser are administered, measured as if by Goldilocks in the den of the Three Bears. Just enough to curb the pain and aid sleep, but not so much as to relax the patient's breathing reflexes into hastened oblivion. The mix has to be just right.

Although I have often seen the before and aftereffects of physical death, I had not witnessed the actual event, always exiting the room as a courtesy of family privacy. The dramatic and sacred second the soul exits the body was still a mystery to me, and not until I faced my own mother's passing would I understand its mystique.

The monitors connected to her oxygen level had been silenced, there would be no need for alarms and codes of resuscitation, or miraculous revivals. The instructions of DNR (do not resuscitate) hung in the room, and she would be allowed to slip into the depths at her own pace.

I watched the numbers of blood oxygenation tell the story. They dropped from the 90's to 80's and lingered awhile in the 70's. This gradual descent allowed a few moments to grasp that this is really happening, "Oh God, this is really happening!" and I jumped from the chair stationed beside her as I called the rest of the family to "hurry, it's happening, hurry!"

The monitor slowed down again, resting at the 50's mark while her breath changed from the rapid shallow pants, to a long slow draw. It was as if she was preparing to 'hold' her breath, causing me to watch intently for it to be pushed out. The rhythm was out of sync, where is the next breath, and would there be a next breath? "Oh God mom, breathe!" and the numbers continued to spiral in reverse symmetry, 46, 42, 38. "It's OK Grandma." Her grandson Eric had entered the room, and took the lead, a calmer head was giving her the 'OK to go' while I cried for my momma. She was leaving, and no amount of my understanding of where she was going would soften the fact that the physical of her would no longer be with me. The routine of her care would no longer be necessary, this part of my life was over, her life here on Earth was over, marked by the lights of the monitor blinking and flashing an indignant red.

There was to be only one last draw of breath, and the relief I felt in this extraordinary act of life would not be followed by another. The subconscious reflex experienced a million times each day was ending, 17, 15, 12. Her granddaughter Chelsea entered this dramatic scene of life and death, and the slow release of air was almost unseen until the machine stayed fixed at 3. She had passed before our very eyes.

The heart had taken its final methodical beat, and the flow of life-giving blood had stopped. The pink blush of her skin would leave in a flow like a wave. It moved across her body, leaving a yellowish tint in its place. I watched it flush across her face, taking the glowing pink color and the lines of worry and pain with it as well.

The essence of her was gone, the light that was my beautiful mother had exited in a softened hush. The tired shell of what was once her, was all that remained. Her body, the worn-out overalls I have often used as an analogy lay in the place of her. It had been shed and left behind, no longer of any use to her, and her spirit was now free to fly unencumbered.

I wish that I could add a caveat here that I had been able to see her soul as she exited to embrace the ones who waited for her. I wanted so badly to see my father there, the partner of her earthly dance. I would have loved to witness the beauty of their story as he took ahold of her hand when they ascended into the ethers. They would be happily together again, and although I know this scene in both my mind and heart, I sincerely wished to have been witness to it, but this was hers alone to enjoy, and she had earned it in all of its splendor.

I had tried to prepare myself, as well as I had prepared her, for the inevitable upcoming journey. I rest assured that at least she was ready. I had done my job as well as I had for any of my patients as she eased into the last of her days. In the end, she was ready to go, and somehow, I had found enough strength within myself to let her.

The Warm Glimpse

There was much grief felt by all who knew Lillian, the beloved Watts Family Matriarch.

The road had been long as she suffered through pain, exhausting breaths and the gradual decline of her treasured independence.

Her exit from this world had been earned, finally shedding the bone, muscle and skin that had served as home to her spirit. Each of us would respond to the loss of her in our own way, but this remarkable dream was reported to me by her grandson Jesse, the night that she passed.

He crawled into bed with tears in his eyes as he whispered to her, telling her that he was happy for her, and that she should be proud of the way she so bravely faced her mortality. He admitted to her that he wasn't one to say prayers, even though he believed in God and prayer itself.

One of the last things he remembered saying before falling into sleep was a promise that he would use her passing as something good in his life. He was going to send all his prayers directly to her, and she could pass them on to where they needed to go.

As he drifted into sleep, he began to see something, it was sky, and he was looking down at a beautiful scene below. His eyes focused on a river of crisp blue water with thick lines of trees on both sides of the expanse. He could see the lush green rounded treetops from high above, the vision was moving, following the river, but he realized that although it was moving, he was not.

He was not flying, although the scene was clearly from the perspective of flying. He knew that he was viewing this scene through another's eyes. He knew that somehow, he had tapped into the vision or reality of what his Grandmother was doing now, and what she was seeing and processing.

At that exact moment in time he was in complete sync with her as she shared a glimpse of the Other Side, in all of its beauty and splendor. She was showing him her complete freedom, and that she was no longer encumbered with illness and pain, but free to fly and explore.

He saw beautiful white light begin to pour into the picture, until the scene was completely engulfed in its brightness and warmth, and then Jesse sat straight up in his bed, excitedly saying "Grandma, I saw it!"

It was beyond a simple dream, and he knew that something precious had been given him. Through his open and loving heart, she had managed to share a glimpse of the beyond, and her personal journey into the light. She was still teaching valuable lessons from the beyond, a gift that he could hold onto and treasure, from the grandma he loved and adored.

"I am only in the next room."

2

After-Life Communication

A Slow Start

Oh, to pull the covers over my head and stay in my lovely dream. I was going to participate in some kind of a race, a school thing, an activity for those approaching a graduation. My mother was there, sitting amongst other parents in support of their children. It was crowded and all of us involved were dressed and ready to run, but for some reason there was a starting delay, and although we had been assigned placement numbers, the delay caused many of us to leave our assigned spots.

Now, when the gun went off to start the race, I was goofing off with a group of friends who had received higher numbers and were to start much farther down the line. I knew instantly that I had sacrificed my early placement and would spend much of the race trying to catch-up to the spot where I 'should' have been. I felt like my mother would be disappointed in my thoughtlessness about losing the important spot and time. I had held an advantage, but I was now in the back in the pack, fighting for each step in the carved and narrow trail.

I decided to break out of the pack to make up some time, veering off of the intended track.

Several others followed, and we found ourselves on an obstacle course, and a much harder road to get to the finish line. But along this route were many different things to try, and I found myself conquering new things.

There were parts of this path, that were extremely hard and required those of us who remained, to work together to get to the top. One was needed to hold the rope for the other, which really slowed us down, but the speed of the race seemed to become secondary now. The feeling of comradery took over, and we were helping one another out beyond the chiseled lines of the trail.

When I finally approached the finish line, I saw my mother, who was still sitting on the bench waiting for me to arrive. The parking lot was empty, as all of the other parents and students had finished and left. Ohhh boy, I thought, I had been thoughtless of my mother who I'm sure had better things to do but wait for me. I approached her apologetically. "Sorry Mom, I kinda' got hung up out there," but she did not scold me as she had a right to do. Instead, she spoke to me in a patient and loving voice and asked me what my number had been.

Fearing her disappointment in me, I reached for the paper that dangled around my neck and showed her the number 8 that had been written with a dark marking pen. She reached out to hold it her hands, and as she touched it, the number began to move and stretch itself out, creating more of a design.

The number 8 now resembled the artful emblem for INFINITY. She lovingly cupped her fingers under my chin and looked directly into my eyes, and I truly focused on her face, yes, she was my mother, the same loving mother I had always known before her death almost four years ago. She held INFINITY in one hand and my face in the other, and she simply said, "This is how long I would wait for you."

John Doe #2

Can one cry tears of grief and loss, and at the same time be filled with the wonder of receiving a message from beyond this world? YES.

It has been a week filled with the task of clearing out a life, you know the dusty tax records and trinkets left behind. This was my task, my brothers unable to face these objects collected and saved, the physical summation of our mother's life.

There was a special file drawer that contained mementos of my father, gone for so very long, almost fifty years now. I approached this drawer with a heavy heart, for it would be almost impossible to let most of this go. I gathered myself and continued until I discovered an envelope that was pushed to the very back of the drawer, it had not been touched for almost as long as his absence. It was marked 'Coroner's office contents of John Doe #2'.

A bolt had sheared, and a scaffolding holding three men 100 feet in the air, tipped and spilled them to their untimely end. Five children and his widow would have to move forward without him, the loss still hard to bear some 49 years later.

I hold this envelope with trepidation, what would his pockets have held, the simple objects that fell with him on that tragic day. I dumped the items into my lap, finding two quarters dating 1965 and 1967, and what was left of his leather tool belt. The belt had either ripped away on impact, or perhaps cut from his broken body. And then I spotted his watch, the band so damaged I dropped it back into my lap and began to sob, the sum of what his body went through on that fateful day. What were his thoughts in the seconds that ticked by, knowing it was the end?

I gathered myself and put the contents back into the envelope, slipping it into my purse unable to process any more, and returned to my home. I continued with life stuff, making dinner, doing dishes etc. Somewhere in the fog of these simple tasks the thought of the watch remained, and I knew I would have to take a closer look because it would reveal the exact time my father left this earth.

Almost a full day passed before I could make myself face this, but by late afternoon I pushed out the routine of the day. I was ready to revisit a hot August afternoon in 1969, and the very minute my life and so many other lives were so irrevocably changed.

With my eyes closed, my fingers rummaged through the contents of the envelope, searching only for the watch crystal, and I placed it squarely in my hand, taking a deep breath before opening my eyes. In that moment, a miracle happened... this old broken watch began to tick. The second hand began to move, right before my eyes, I could not believe it as I watched it climb from the bottom of the clock, circling passed the 12 mark and passing the 2 before it stopped.

This watch was no miraculous tricked out digital and technical wonder of modern age, but a simple working man's wind up Timex from the days of long ago. How could this be? Its slogan came to mind,

"Takes a lickin' and keeps on tickin' " but seriously, after 49 years, and with the extreme *lickin'* it took?

I held this precious artifact in my hand and my tears changed from those of grief and loss, to a warm awareness. I realized that what I held here was more than the measure of when a life ended, but a special message from him, the father that meant so very much to me, that his life continued on, and that it always would.

The Number 432

If you want to find the secrets of the Universe, think in terms of energy, frequency and vibration.

- Nikola Tesla

A few years ago, I began to notice the number 432. It would show up in my dreams, the numbers floating in the air around my bed. Many times, I would look up during a car ride just in time to see a road sign sporting 432, or it was printed on the license plate traveling in front of me. The number became prevalent in my awareness, I was supposed to pay attention, not knowing it would soon play an important role in my life.

During this awareness, a Facebook post popped up about the importance of geometry, and how the number 432 plays a pivotal role in what is called sacred geometry. Math had never been my strong suit, and I was completely unfamiliar with it, but knew I had to get to the bottom of why I was having these promptings.

I googled *'geometry 432'* and was surprised at what I found, and the lesson it taught me.

'The language of Frequency in Sonic Geometry is 432. It is derived from the mathematical basis of a sonic pitch also known as the philosophical pitch, and it is in perfect balance with Nature and the Universe.

432Hz will fill you with a sense of peace and well-being, it will resonate within your body, release emotional blockages, take you to a natural relaxation state, and expand your consciousness.

432Hz will make your body and the organic world which surrounds it, resonate in a natural way. HZ works at the heart chakra, and therefore could have a good influence on your spiritual progression.'

Shortly after this discovery I became very busy as my mother's health began to decline, and a few weeks after she passed away, I had the following dream:

I saw my mother laying in a bed on 'the Other Side' though it was not the hospital bed I had become accustomed to seeing her in, but more of a special healing berth. It was completely encompassed in the beautiful light that surrounded her.

I was made to know that she was in recovery and being assisted in a type of soul hospital, and that I should not worry, as this was not unusual. My mother's earthly body had greatly deteriorated before her passing, thus affecting her ethereal, spiritual body, and she was in the process of being healed. I was also made to know that she needed guidance out of the box in her thinking so to speak. After so many years of rigorous religious training, she was locked into a tight mindset, and she was having a great deal of difficulty releasing herself from it.

After you pass, there is a lot to remember about who you really are, and the depth and magnificence of our true home. Great care is given, and answers are revealed at a pace that each individual soul is able to accept and hold. Letting go of the limiting earthly teachings can be difficult, but in the afterlife, there is the greatest love and thoughtfulness offered while nursing a soul into remembrance, and it is done in the gentlest manner of service and care.

As I saw her in this bed of light, I just knew that she wanted to communicate with me but could not. I could feel the distance between us and I started to call out to her, trying to close the gap. My face was tilted upwards, and my hand was cupped around my mouth trying to amplify the sound of my voice. "Mom you need to lower your vibrational frequency to 432 to be able to talk to me."

As I shouted towards her I thought, 'I can't believe that I am yelling as if she is in the next room, but I raised my voice as if being louder would help, and I continued anyway, "Mom, I am going to work to raise my frequency level to 432 and if you work to lower yours, I know we will be able to talk to each other" and with that, I woke up still talking about a 432 frequency, and vibrational levels…and other things that I knew nothing about. And I noticed… that I still had my hand cupped at my mouth.

I can still recall in rich detail, the entirety of the dream, and the peace that it gave me knowing what was happening to her on the Other Side. She was receiving the care that she needed, and I decided that I needed to learn more about frequency and vibration.

We would eventually close the gap between our two worlds, having given each other an important clue as how we could do it, and we were both willing to do the work.

Just a Phone Call Away

Strange how a simple phone call can change a perspective in the world as you know it.

This morning I was doing normal chores, and I thought I heard a familiar ring tone, yes, it was my phone, and wouldn't you know it, I was a flight of stairs away. Could I make it downstairs in time? Probably not, but I did try, taking a step forward, finding myself tangled in a ball of yarn that had fallen out of the bag I was carrying. Giant loops of it had enveloped my shoe and for the life of me I could not get myself loose. I laughed as I said aloud "Well I guess I wasn't supposed to answer that one," and continued to unravel myself, the situation notably funny but not a big deal, I will just call them back.

But this call could would not be so easily returned.

You see, the phone posted the caller as MOM, and in times past this would have been totally normal, a call from my Mom saying, "hi hon just calling to say hello, what-cha-doing?"

But this kind of call from my mother would never come again, she has passed to a seemingly unreachable place, and I cannot count the many times I have picked up the phone, wanting so much to call her, and then sadly remembering that impossibility.

I was having lunch with my husband the day before, when I noticed an elderly woman being guided into a seat by one of the women accompanying her. I couldn't help but notice the attentive care given by the younger of the two. She helped her read the menu and offer suggestions for her meal, adjusted the straw in her glass, unfolded her napkin, and when her food arrived, she made sure the plate was not too hot before she cut her food into manageable bites. It was the kind of care that I can proudly claim to have given my own mother as her health declined, and in watching these kind acts so freely given, I began to feel a tightness in my throat. I missed my Mom.

As I put on my coat to leave I leaned over to their table and whispered, "you sure made me miss my Mom today" and I touched my heart as we exchanged smiles. I began to ask if the young woman was a professional caregiver but before I could finish the question she said, "just a granddaughter" and I told her she was beautiful in her selfless acts of kindness.

I thought of my mother a few more times than usual that afternoon, remembering the fun we always had together. She would giggle at my spur of the moment suggestion of "let's go do something" and we would set off to lunch or the dollar movie. She loved the attention and the 'naughtiness' of leaving the chores behind and chasing fun in the middle of the day.

Life moves on, and it will be four years this summer without hearing my mother's voice on the other end of the phone, and so I marveled at the missed call today marked MOM.

I had not deleted her number in my contacts, instead, I took over her phone number after she passed, unusual you might say, but this was the same number given our family in 1957. I grew up with that number, assured that when I dialed the numbers in the correct sequence, I would hear her familiar voice on the other end of the line. Now that she has passed, I still use this familiar group of number's as my own, thus keeping them valid and alive and still in the family.

I hold a phenomenon in my hand, a wonder in its own right in its compact size and the capability of connecting here to there across the globe, but now I marvel, as this is so much more. This is *'miracle'* kind of stuff, as I read the precious word lit up across the screen, MOM, and I know that this call has traveled so much further.

I sat in a peaceful stillness as I continued to look at the word MOM, and I questioned how my phone could call itself. There had been no accidental redial here alone in my home and on an entirely different floor.

I stared at the word until I could see it no more, my eyes spilling into a mix of tears, those of a missed loved one, but also with gratitude and incredible joy. This phone call was an undeniable gift, a contact, and a hello from the beyond.

Dare I redial? Maybe she would answer, and I listened with hope as the line clicked into oblivion.

She had felt my longing from so very far away, and she had found a way to answer back. She was still there on the other end of the unseen line between us, and she would always be.

Perhaps oblivion is really not so very far away, maybe just as far as phone call.

Artistic Impressions

There are people who leave lasting impressions, and I lament the loss of one who left a forever impression on me. I was young and malleable when I met Ron, the eldest of the Clayton brothers, he was handsome and interesting and he offered a more experienced and worldly view to me and his younger brother Clair.

He had recently returned from the army, bringing home Yung Cha, his Korean bride, and he was busy working toward an art degree at the University of Utah. He would eventually become my brother-in-law and we spent a lot of time together as married couples. I learned much about life and art from Ron, always in his element in his studio amongst his newest art installations.

I still remember my laughter as he showed me that yes, there really was a color named 'baby shit brown.'

I saw my first Picasso with him on a trip to the University of California at Berkeley, and found that vacationing with purposeful planned visits to galleries and museums could be fun. I also noticed that fun was something that Ron did not allow himself much of. He seemed to be haunted by self-esteem issues, and he over compensated by appearing overly pompous and heady as he chased academic acceptance. It took time and trust for him to share some of the experiences that brought him to this limiting headspace.

In high school he was often accosted by a bully, not another student, as Ron could certainly take care of himself, but an over-zealous assistant principal who seemingly had it in for Ron. He accused him of being useless and lazy and would never amount to much in this life. I wish I could say that this was a calculated and honorable approach meant to motivate him, but this was not the case; his intentions were personal and he was accomplished at getting into Ron's head. All of his future achievements were a defiant fist in the air to this man, and he would work his entire life to surpass the expectations of both him and his own imposed self-doubt.

Ron accomplished an art degree and earned a tenured college professorship. His art is recognized and saluted amongst his peers; it seems he had conquered this demon from his past, though he rarely let himself fully enjoy his own successes.

A few weeks after Ron passed into the afterlife, I tried to contact him, curious if he was OK, and I called out to him by name. After many tries, I got a visual of an old black and white TV, the screen was full of static and grey snow and written across it were the words, *Technical Difficulties. Please Stand By.*

I knew I had received a message from him, although he was not quite ready to converse. Leave it to Ron to send such a creative message to convey what he could not yet say.

Almost another month would past before I received this wonderful contact dream of him.

The setting was a quaint café on a rainy afternoon. My attention was drawn towards the back of the establishment, and to a large padded corner booth that held at least six patrons, with another seated on a chair in the aisle.

I recognized Ron immediately sitting against the darkened window with an ease I had never seen in this life. The smile on his face was easy and light, and he no longer looked like he carried the weight of the world on his shoulders. Next to him were the art world's finest, both past and present. He was keeping company with the creators of the works he admired, studied and taught. I watched with an honored fascination at being allowed to see a man who was finally in his element and being accepted for who he was and what he had to offer.

He was among true peers, and they sat together as friends and equals. Van Gogh, Matisse, Jackson Pollock, Georgia O Keefe, and others that I didn't recognize outright. In these close darkened quarters, Ron looked happier than I had ever seen him before. I was so enthralled in the scene, an inspired setting for an illustrious painting in its own right. Talented comrades, sharing company, and bouts of requited laughter, while drinking thick black coffee as the air around them filled with the smoke of endless unfiltered cigarettes.

Thank You Ron, for this cherished vision, I will carry it always. I wish you well as you go forward in grateful appreciation for the life lessons you shared with me here, and from the beyond.

Talladega Nights and Other Gatherings

Looking through photo books, I was reminded of many family camping trips and excursions. The memories were thick as I thumbed through photos of dirty faced kids holding up soda cans, and of Mom standing in front of the old Coleman stove.

There was someone missing in our family photos. My father had always been the one behind the camera, leaving us with a sad discovery after his sudden death, that there was to be little physical evidence of him. His face would be committed to our memories, and we found ourselves lucky to see the shadow of his likeness cast on the ground in front of those of us smiling and saying "cheese."

Understandably, pictures had become a big deal to my mother, and it was important to get everyone included in them. I understood her need for these physical mementos, and she would often say, "You never know when it will be the last time." My sister proved this statement to be true as her earthly existence was terminated in literal moments as well. Mom had good reason to document as much of our lives as she could. My brother Dave surprised her one Christmas with a shiny new camera fit for the digital age, and she would snap photos while happily schmoozing at family gatherings.

Camping tonight after a full day of rain in the Uinta mountains, my husband plugged in the generator so we could watch a movie as we snuggled in the warmth of the trailer.

Talladega Nights and the annals of Ricky Bobbie filled my head and dreams of nothingness until a picture came into view pushing everything else away. It was a vivid living picture of one of our family gatherings, and each of us were being directed to stand in front of a large flowering tree in my mother's front yard.

I enjoyed watching the antics, trying to wrangle us into a row, "nope too long, I can't get everyone in, form a second row, and kids, you all line up together in front, better, now squish together, come on act like you like each other" and the camera would start clicking away.

The photographer would be changed out occasionally, making sure that all of us were included in the scene, and as I took my turn with the camera, I thought about who was missing in our family photo. I found myself looking for orbs of light that are sometimes seen in photos.

I have read of this phenomenon and believe it is possible, but I had never experienced it in any of my own photo's.

It was at this time that I saw two balls of light come into view and wedge softly into place within the group. Watching through the camera's lens, I saw the orbs began to change into a kind of a glowing smudgy oval and I could make out two more smiling faces saying cheese within the group. My father and my sister had joined the rest of us in the photo, and a distinct feeling came over me in what I will call a 'knowing'. I had just witnessed a confirmation from our loved ones who had passed, reaffirming their continued presence in our family, and with a complete awareness of our lives.

Not the Strong Stuff

From time to time, I go through the pages of my dream journals. I love the affirmation of the wonders I have been witness to, and how far I have come in the discovery of my own self during spirit lessons. I came across this conversation with my mother almost a year after she passed, and knew I was supposed to include it here.

The wonder of 'hearing' a loved one from the Other Side is a something that I do not take lightly. I am used to my own thoughts but this is something else, and it sounds and feels completely different.

There are times when the conditions are 'just right' to hear, and one of those times is while I am cruising on an open dirt trail on my ATV. The roar of the engine lulls me into a hypnotic, and open state of mind with my thoughts safely cocooned within the helmet.

This day as I rode, I thought of the times I had been able to contact my sister in this way, and I decided to try to reach my mother. I called out to her, saying that I missed her and needed her, and after a few minutes, she responded and I HEARD HER!

"You're not ridings horses" and it made me laugh out loud as this had been an on-going joke between us when her phone calls went to voicemail. I would listen to the recording of her saying, "Where are you now? Hiking, bike riding or out riding horses?" always followed by her familiar haha. It truly was the perfect introduction to this new way of communicating.

"You are really here Mom?" stating the obvious, and she told me that she would always be there for me when I needed her.

I asked her if she was OK, and she answered, "Oh yes, much better now" adding "at first it was hard, and I didn't understand it all, I thought things were supposed to be one way and when they were not how I was expecting them to be, I was confused."

She talked about how she had to learn to let go of teachings and promises she had relied on her whole life. She had lived a perfect example of faithful living within structured religious beliefs.

She had to be eased into remembering the depth and magnitude of her own soul.

When I asked her if she had really been able to let it go, I got a distinct visual of a hand, and my first thought was that it reminded me of the opening scene in the TV series 'SIX FEET UNDER.'

A closed hand is extended, and then the fingers pop open quickly as the hand retracts. I understood this as a sign of release, and her letting go of earthly faith and beliefs, to be able to progress and move forward in her spiritual journey.

I asked her if she had talked to Dad yet and her answer gave me much insight into how far she had progressed, as she explained that yes eventually she would, "but as you know," she said, "he is really into his studies." This was huge, because ever since he passed in 1969, she has held tightly onto the idea that he was just waiting for her to come home to him, and that he kept himself busy by building the perfect abode for all of the family to continue what had been lost when he died.

She explained that although she and my father would always be connected, she had accepted that this was not exactly the way. After much loving care, she was able to understand that there is so much more to the afterlife than religion had offered.

She went on to say, that I should not forget that my father's love for us was for all of time, and she knew that our families sacrifice of losing him early, was all a part of a plan they had made together. She and my father had a contractual agreement "to help each other" and further explained that "ALL WAS IMPORTANT" and she had needed to remember this first, before seeing him.

I asked about my sister Kaylyn, had she spent much time with her? She said that yes, they had spent as much time together as they could, but offered that "she is deep into service, and she is so happy to be involved in an important work," and my mother said she was proud of her in this effort, and that she knew that she would be able to see her, if, and when she needed to.

I understood all she was saying, though I was a bit dismayed at her not having the kind of contact with my dad and sister as I thought she would, but she assured me that everything was as it should be, and that she was very happy.

She had conveyed a lot of deep information, but I was not quite ready to let her go and asked her "Mom, what is Heaven really like?" She answered in the same word game that Kaylyn uses, giving me an unfamiliar word that both answers the question and leaves evidentiary proof. I am reassured that our conversation was real when I am pushed to look up an unfamiliar word for its meaning: RESPLENDENT.

The trail was beginning to get treacherous and I knew it was time for our goodbyes. She assured me that she would always be there for me when I needed her, and we were expressing our love for each other when she began to giggle, saying "and about those mimosa's, have one for me!" with another giggle.

I was completely gob-smacked, as this was NOT something my mother would have ever even thought about in this life, she had never tasted or even smelled alcohol. A picture of a bottle of champagne came to mind and she immediately said "no" as if she could see the picture too, saying "mimosa, with the orange juice, not the strong stuff" and I had to laugh along with her. This was so out of character for my earthly mother, she had really come a long way, showing me by this statement alone that she had in fact, let so much of the old behaviors go.

Resplendent: Splendid, Magnificent, Brilliant, Dazzling, Glittering, Gorgeous, Impressive, Imposing, Spectacular, Striking, Stunning, Majestic, 'having a very bright or beautiful appearance'

Thanks Mom, for such a vivid experience and giving me such a perfectly descriptive word for Heaven, RESPLENDENT.

Blocking Grief

As a hospice volunteer, I have learned that grief has its own expression, from the stoic family leader who never gives in to tears, to the completely distraught. The lesson is there is no right or wrong way to grieve.

Since my own NDE experience, I am genuinely happy for those who have returned home, knowing that their mission here has been accomplished. But for those of us left behind, there is a recognition that nothing in this world will ever be the same, and the enjoyment of life together in the physical is over. There will be no more shared dinners, movies, phone calls or warm hugs, and there is much grief in accepting this new reality.

When I lost my father at sixteen, I faced a life-sized regret of not dancing with him at my junior high school graduation. I was young and stupid, thinking my friends would call me a nerd, and I will never forget the rejected look on his face when I refused. Only months later he was gone, and my never being able to feel his strong hands or his whiskers against my cheek was unbearable to me.

I spent years praying for a visit, or a dream about him, and realized that I was beginning to forget what his voice had even sounded like. I would cry during movies that involved a father/child relationship even years after what some would deem it beyond time enough to get over it.

For anyone who is struggling with their grief, I offer support, because your grief is important, it is real, and it is yours to have with no explanation necessary or a timetable to be measured by.

But…. may I also offer that I have learned that the intensity of my grief was exactly what was keeping those very dreams and visits from coming to me. It was some forty years since his passing before I learned that my tears and dismay were a physical block that kept him away from me. The dreams hadn't come, and so my tears didn't stop, and it was all such a never-ending cycle that took years to get turned in the other direction.

I quote from a book written by Galen Stoller called 'my life after life' surprisingly written AFTER he was killed in a horrific accident. His son's words from the Other Side were captured by his father Dr. Paul Stoller, who learned to 'hear' him from the beyond. His son told him that he had tried many times to reach his mother, but that her grief was keeping her from hearing him. She was not receptive and open, and he was unable to break through into her dreams, and he had all but given up trying.

His father on the other hand was open and listening, feeling it was completely possible, and he was able to hear his son. Because his father had accepted and believed, his son made it a point to come to him often, and their connection grew stronger, creating a bridge to one another.

It had now been many months since my sister Kaylyn passed, and with my husband out of town, I was alone, and it was a perfect time to express the grief I still held. I decided to try to connect with her, truly believing I could. I had meditated earlier and made my intentions known, and in bed that evening I called out to her by name. I lit a candle and asked her over and over to please come into my dreams, until I eventually fell asleep.

I woke in the middle of the night so disappointed, she had not come, and I called out to her again and asked why she would not come to me. I talked aloud to her, reminding her of the pain we had both gone through in losing our father. Now that she had left too, she should have a very good idea how cruel it feels to miss someone so much and not get a visitation, or at least a confirmation that they were alright.

We had made promises that we would come to each other, and I reached my hands in the air towards a spot on the ceiling to send my sad intentions to. I cried out loud, "Please show up" and I looked for even a spot of light or a tiny flicker, so I would know she was there. It did not happen, though I continued for hours as I watched that corner of the ceiling, alone in my candle lit room, before finally falling asleep.

The following days were filled with life stuff, but I still held out hope that she would come to me. I attended a physic fair and got a reading from a talented medium who was spot on in what she relayed to me from the beyond. Without any prompting she had known that I was looking for two passed loved ones, male and female and she brought me such peace as she opened memories and spoke of things only my sister would know about.

I knew she had truly connected with her, as she mentioned things that I did not know at the time. I later confirmed with her children, that they were true, thus offering confirmation that my sister had really communicated from the beyond.

Towards the end of the reading, the medium said that my sister wanted to talk about 'that night' and I knew exactly the one she was referring to. She said the thing that I had asked her to do was not possible, and that she just couldn't do what I asked, because both my grief and her skill level would not allow it. She wanted me to know that she knew of my distress and tears for her, and that she HAD come, and was doing her best to comfort me. She told me that she had wrapped her arms around me and laid next to me throughout the night, wiping the tears off of my cheeks.

The reading gave me a new hope that it was possible to reach her, and I began to focus on our relationship instead of her death. I stopped watching the calendar days of her birthday or death date, and the intensity of my grief began to level off.

Please understand that I will never stop grieving the physical loss of her, but now I remember the life we spent together, instead of focusing on her departure, and this has helped bridge the stop gap between us.

We have both grown in our communicational skills, and I have been able to reach her many times now, and when I ask if she is still there, she tells me that she will be there whenever I need her to be.

It has been seven years now since her passing, and of course I still miss her, but maybe it is just in the knowing that it is possible to reach her, that has helped me level off my need to.

I don't try to contact her as often anymore, I have no doubt that she lives on and is doing important work, she is fulfilled, and I am still here to finish whatever my purpose is.

I am carrying on as she would wish me to, but I confess that I sleep better knowing there are nights when she comes to check on me and wraps me up in her arms.

YES, I know this is possible.

The Missing State of Delaware

When one passes, you cannot help but reminisce, reliving memories of time spent together. It happens during mundane duties of life stuff, when you grasp a wonderful stolen moment of reflection. Sometimes these moments arrive unexpectedly, overflowing and spilling out from the place in your heart where they now reside.

It had been weeks since my mother passed, and as I went through her effects, I came across a collection. It was of every state's minted quarter, held together in a folded cardboard carrier. Every now and then, a new state would be released, and my mother would look through her change until she could fill another empty spot on the board. I had no idea she was doing this, but at the time of her death, she had collected all but the state of Delaware. I made a mental note of this while showing it to my husband and then put the collection away for safe keeping.

Months later, when the anniversary of her birthday came, I was feeling quite melancholy, and my husband decided to break my somber mood by taking me out for ice cream. It was a sweet gesture as this is something she and I would sneak off to do together, and it seemed a perfect tribute to her today.

We were trapped in a slow line, with cars both in front of us and behind. We were stuck with no place to go, and so we looked for something to do. We were using the car wash linen to wipe down the dash and cup holders when I noticed the ashtray full of coins, and I started sifting through pennies, nickels and dimes for the grandbabies piggy banks.

There were three quarters to be put in the slot for the parking meter and I had already placed two, when a thought hit me to look for the missing state of my mother's collection. Yes, you are right dear reader, I could not have scripted a more fitting celebration of her that day, as we clinked our malts together in the form of cheers and happy birthday wishes, while I held on tightly to a quarter minted for the United States of Delaware.

Happenstance, Coincidence, Serendipity, call it what you will, but all seemed quite of accidental perfection to me here at the ice cream shop that she loved, while holding the exact coin that would complete her collection on this special day of remembering her. Perfect.

Coincidental Message

I have written before of my angel sister Kaylyn, who passed away almost seven years ago now.

I miss her happy smile and the sound of her voice, but since her passing, she has played an intricate part in my increasing spiritual awareness, and she is still very instrumental in my lessons of life-after-life communication.

A few years ago, I sat in my office scrolling through photos of her, it was her birthday, and I was reflecting on her life. The phone rang, and as a real estate agent, I gathered myself to answer the call.

It was from an agent in another state, and she said that she had many questions about the booming Utah market, and could I spare a few moments. "Sure" I said, and we ended up talking for quite a while, her personality was outgoing and fun, and we shared some realtor funnies.

Towards the end of our conversation she confessed that she had looked at several other agent's websites before calling me. She told me that she just had a good feeling about me, and I reciprocated, telling her that I had enjoyed our conversation, and that I was glad that she had picked me. I asked for her name and contact information in hopes we could share some referral business in the future.

She had started to give me her name when the line buzzed and became crackly, making her name sound foreign. I wasn't sure that I had heard it correctly, and so I asked her to spell it out, and I began to write the letters down, one after the other K...A...Y...L...Y...N and I repeated them aloud, as I wrote them down, K A Y L Y N, until I recognized what I had just written. Shocked, I asked her in a confused whisper, "Your name is Kaylyn"? "Yes" she said, "Kaylyn," and I could not help the surprise in my voice and I started to cry. I looked down at the paper where I had just written my sister's name, while her face looked back at me from the pictures on my computer screen.

I began to share the amazing synchronicity of the timing of her call, and their sharing of an unusual name, when she stopped me and said, "there are no accidents." She went on to tell me that she had felt compelled take a moment on this day to make the call that had been scribbled on her to do list. They were just basic questions, but she had followed an urge to call me above all of the agents on her list.

The coincidence was not lost on either one of us, we knew without a doubt, that my sister had orchestrated this phone call from the stranger with the uncommon name of Kaylyn. I had needed, and received, a wonderful Hello from Heaven, a call made to me... from Kaylyn, on her birthday.

3

The Importance of Dreams

*"Answers are meaningless
to those who are not asking questions."*

Dear reader, I wanted to include a few notes about dreams, because they are more important to our lives than we had ever dreamed (pun intended.)

Dreams are so much more than just something to keep the mind occupied while the body recuperates. Dreams are an important connection to spirit, our guides and angels and to our highest self without the conflicting mind chatter of the day. It is a time when our subconscious is receptive to the assessments of the soul's desires.

We can and do visit our spiritual home and loved ones in our dreams, the work is learning to retain the messages after waking. This has been such a huge part of my quest, and after years of practice, I still have to work every morning to retain and record them.

I am including examples of brain wave charts, as an introduction to the varying stages of relaxation and sleep. Part of my research has been holding onto longer periods of pre-sleep, or the Alpha and Theta waves, because I have found myself more accessible to seeing and hearing from loved ones from the Other Side during this time.

This cat-nap stage is generally when I hear heavenly messages or will catch myself speaking in a language that I am not familiar with in this lifetime. Generally, this stage lasts for only a few moments or as long as seven minutes, allowing for a quick nap. This is when you experience the feeling of falling or jerking as you begin to let yourself go. You have entered a state of in-between wake and sleep, and it is a wonderful time of openness to receive.

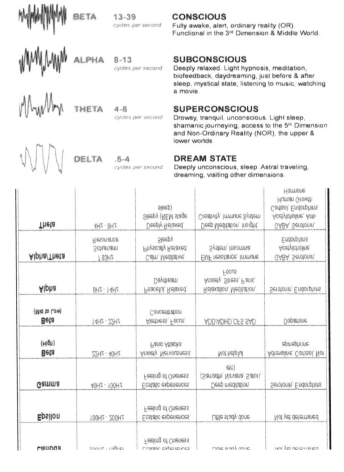

I try to retain this period for as long as possible or will generally wake myself up again to repeat this stage several times before allowing myself to completely fall asleep. This is one way I have learned to control my sleep, and I am completely relaxed when finally falling into the deep sleep and dream stages of Delta brain waves.

I do not proclaim myself as a scientific expert here, but I have studied the components of brain waves. I have been experimenting on myself for many years, keeping my findings in my bedside journals. The human brain is a marvelous wonder, and the stages of its access though sleep are spiritual in nature and a direct conduit to the Higher Power.

A Very Personal Effect

Dreams are a very personal effect and a blessing when they are restful and beautiful. You wake feeling warm and joyful when you have spent the night visiting with a departed loved one, or the total freedom from life's anxieties as you lift off and fly over treetops and sandy beaches. You get to see the world from a new perspective through dreams, even in the terrifying ones that push you to turn on the lights to stave off the darkness.

Dreams can just seem silly and confusing, as people that you know so well can act differently or even inappropriately. Their appearance can change to someone younger, and it pulls us back in time, and into long forgotten situations.

Some people remember their dreams while others say they do not. Their mind snaps instantly awake, pushing out the night's fog. There are things to do in the day ahead, and they jump into business, feeling the world of dreams unimportant and just a nonsensical mind release.

In my early years of recognizing vivid and lucid dreams, I would lay silently in the darkness, working to remember and retain them. I would allow them to run through my head, while I searched for their meaning. I held onto them long enough to be able to reach for my bedside journal to capture them, or at least note key words to bring them back at a later time.

I still practice this art, as my dreams have assisted in my learning much about myself, and I have gained wondrous spiritual knowings through them. In the beginning I took my dreams too literally, rather than looking at possible interpretations or symbolisms. It was not until I began to listen to my own intuition, that I would realize that many of the situations and people who were in them were simply symbolic representations. They were playing a part to denote a troubled area or things I should be paying attention to.

Many of my teaching dreams come with a heading of *'Parable'* or *'Metaphor'* posted on a large billboard, so I will take notice. Nothing is left to the chance of misinterpretation or misrepresentation. Some dreams are seemingly just dreams of sand as I call them, the ones that fall into dust as soon as you wake, and little can be done to pull them back into something solid enough to examine or view again. I have learned to tell the difference.

I do have prophetic dreams of possible future events, but when I have them, I am usually accompanied by a guide or a loved one who has passed, and the setting is one of teacher and student. My angel sister was my first teacher from the Other Side, she came to me in a dream, and after making sure that I was focused and ready, she showed me that a new way of the world was coming into the light. She showed me a time that peace would prevail, and money would no longer be a focus. Any laws if needed would be made in the light of God, and those of dark intent would been shown as such, and no longer able to hide behind deflection and lies. She reminded me before she left, that this was important, saying "pay attention to this." When both she and my guide make sure that I am indeed paying attention, I know that I am going to wake with pertinent information.

Our guides will nudge us as we sleep, but they do not openly 'tell' us what's what. I have been asked "Why?" The answer is 'our free will' and it is important. This is our ride, our experience, and our journey. Although much is offered to assist us along the way, we do not have to take the hand that is presented. We are not wrong in deciding to go off course at times, as that is our choice and why we are here.

Although there is a predetermined road map with many check points when we are born, there are many roads that will lead us to our desired destination. Our loving guides will continue to give us nudges to assist us, but never is an answer just given without a sincere asking of the question. That would be considered interference, and an affront to our free will.

One of my favorite sayings came to me one early morning as I lay quietly before rising, simply stated, it said *"answers are meaningless to those who are not asking questions."*

I have spent many years asking questions with a determined heart, and it has taken all of those years to prepare myself for the answers I now receive. I am finally confident in my understanding and the representations that the dreams pose. If you are sincere, just be patient, and never stop asking.

The Boy I Knew

Last night's dream was of a much younger version of myself, my romantic heart was in a vulnerable place. A boy I loved and cared about for most of my life played a part in this dream, he was rejecting me, something that had never happened in real life. His demeanor was cold, and he callously ignored my dismay and tears, as I questioned why he no longer returned my affection. How could he change his mind so suddenly?

There were faceless friends around me, all with my best interests at heart, they were trying to take me away from the situation, to another party, or another boy, but I was having none of it. I was stuck in my own disbelief, shedding tears attached with hope, that somehow, he would change back to the person I once knew, and that he would love me again. I could not move on until I was sure that it was completely over and finished. I let the 'other' opportunities pass me by, and because I was not ready I did not move forward and I did not progress, I was stagnant.

The dream advanced to another day, and nothing had magically changed. I stood in the same place, looking at the one I deeply cared for, but there was no return in his eyes, what had been there before was gone. I looked at him one last time as I said a quiet and personal goodbye within myself. It was time for me to move on, and so I left without looking back. I was finally ready to find what else awaited me.

As I lay in the dark, going over the dream I was confused at first. Why after so many years was I dreaming of this first love? Initially, I looked at the literal meaning of the dream, was something not yet settled between us? Was unhappiness or problems in my marriage to come?

Going over the scenarios, I heard a soft voice tell me "he is only a representation" and immediately the pieces of many dream puzzles fell into place. He was the best representation to show me changes that I was not yet ready for. Because he had always offered stability in his caring for me, he was perfect for the part to teach me that although I do not like it, changes will occur, and there will be nothing that I can do about it. There is a time to let it go and move forward and it is hard to let something go that has always offered stability and comfort, but it is necessary for our continued growth.

Another vivid dream came to mind, showing a version of myself in rapid waters and holding onto the jagged edge of a rushing creek. I was using all of my strength to hold onto the rocks, I was exhausted, and fear and despair was all that I had left. It was inevitable that the current would eventually pull me off, but I continued to struggle using nothing but shear will. If I continued to hold on, I would have nothing left to help me navigate myself through the water and I would most likely perish. I heard "let go, do not fight with that which draws you, this is what you asked for, let go of the safety of what you know, you will be alright."

It is OK to take the time needed to accept change, cry the necessary tears, but then find strength in the act of wiping them away and moving forward to something else. Life is full of uncertainty and change, and it is not in our own best interest to try to hold onto something long after it is gone. Change is inevitable, and also a catalyst to our growth that will make one stronger in the resolve of finding something better.

Another Dream Scenario

I have learned that sometimes people and places are inserted in dreams for a learning purpose. The dream is not about that person literally, but their familiarity can be used as an example, and a valuable learning tool. The presence of someone familiar keeps the dream from seeming entirely nonsensical, evoking memory or a feeling that makes the dream lesson as real as it can be. Let me explain.

My mother passed away a few years ago. I had been a hospice volunteer for five years, so being at the bedside of someone in their last days was not unusual. But this was my mother, and so these last days were as personal as they could get.

In the end I questioned every one of my decisions in her care, the medicine, the doses, the air tubes, the temperature in the room, all of it. My mother was tired and was no longer invested in the outcome. She had given her care over to me and I had lovingly accepted. But now that she was gone, I spent a lot of time recalling every decision. Had I done everything I could for her? I knew that I had, but I found the what-ifs still clouded my thoughts.

The Dream

My mother (a patient) is in her last hours, and my brother Jeff (playing the role of a distant but concerned member of the family) is pushing me to remove the breathing apparatus, "she's dying" he argued, his voice was elevated," do you really think she would want that thing in her when she dies? Take it out and let her speak or take her own last breaths." His point made sense, but then I, (playing the constant caregiver) who had made all of the decisions without his or any other family member's help, was reluctant, I knew removing this life-giving tube would surely bring a hastening to her end.

Was I ready to let her go? Is this what she would want me to do? What would her choice be?

There was hesitation and strife, stress and indecision, but above all was the anger and fear of the inevitable, and when mixed together it created a toxic dose of stymied reluctance. All was being portrayed in my dream, and then the dream paused... like someone had taken control over the remote. I was able to step out of the vivid illustration far enough to be able to see and feel all sides of this equation. Each family member was loving her in their own way, each looking at a hopeless outcome and the proper steps to get there.

This dream was a valuable lesson for me as I continued my hospice volunteer work.

I had been given a gift of insight into the full range of emotions in a dramatic hospital setting. My mother and my brother were playing a role in the dream to make the scenario as real as possible for me.

Losing a loved one brings on the strongest of emotions. There are hurts that have never quite healed, the appreciation and thank-yous that were never offered, forgiveness never asked for or given, and the unspeakable regrets of lost time.

I will remember and appreciate having felt these emotions from all sides of the family. Now I have a clearer understanding of the behaviors of those being left behind, and the very personal and individual reactions when one seems outwardly unreasonable during the time of hard decisions.

May 29, 2015

This is All We Will Speak of That

I woke from something I will call an interruption of a powerful spirit meeting. I actually leapt from my bed in anger, walking halfway down the hallway while hearing a calm but strong voice of authority. "THIS IS ALL WE WILL SPEAK OF THAT WHICH IS PROVIDENCE!"

I literally woke in a huff of emotion, but I was fully awake as I heard the words... and I stood in confusion as to what I was being told. I knew that whatever it was that I had been asking for, was not going to happen.

I write of it now as I scan through my journals for the last bits and pieces this book will contain. This story is important because although we may not remember our Heavenly visits upon waking, our souls do get spiritual updates from time to time.

The mind working in tune with the soul is what I strive for, I work hard to prove that the physical Claudia can handle spirit information and new pieces of the spiritual puzzle without freaking out, but I did, I freaked out that morning.

I was mad, mad enough to jump from the meeting when the answer was not to my liking, my earth body and soul present for the answer, and I, Claudia, didn't like the answer.

It was a NO, and my abrupt abort of the meeting ended with me waking, standing upright, while still hearing the rebuttal. "THIS IS ALL WE WILL SPEAK OF THAT WHICH IS PROVIDENCE!"

After I calmed down, I looked up the word, as it is not a part of my everyday vernacular... 'PROVIDENCE' I looked up the word, and this came up first:

Providence: Fate, Destiny, Nemesis, Kismet, Predestination, The stars, "The protective care of God or of nature as a spiritual power."

Wow, I was conversing with the realms that actually speak like this. And I now know why they use these unfamiliar terms, it is so we will pay attention and know with complete confidence, that it does not come from our own self when we hear it.

In looking at the very next entry in my dream journal dated a few days later, June 2nd, 2015 it all made perfect sense.

I wrote about a dream of my mother, and how we couldn't find her. Had she been kidnapped or lost? She had not come home and she had never done this before, we were afraid she might be hurt.

I was amped up and ready to 'FIX' anything that was wrong with her. I rallied items including a paint brush and a can of shellac, and I was hell-bent on repairing whatever the problem would be, and then I woke up.

May I offer here that my mother passed on July 9th, 2015, and I just noticed the correlation of the two events as I re-read them in my journal. I realized that at the time of these dreams, I had just 60 days left with her in this world.

I am sure I was asking for extra time with her, maybe already granted once, or even twice before. I can imagine my pleas for her to stay here with me, and not to go "no not yet, please, I need more time," but time had run out, and I was not happy with the answer I received. I don't like no's, but then does anyone?

There was nothing left to do but accept the inevitable and to cease my pleading, the answer had been clearly given, and there would be no reprieves, and so this is all we will speak of that which is Providence.

Of Black Elk and Dreams

In my first book, *GIFTS FROM THE EDGE Stories of the Other Side,* I mentioned the coincidence of both my son and I reading the book *Black Elk Speaks* by John G. Neihardt at exactly same time. We are blood descendants of the Catawba Indian Nation, and the fact that this book was not a new release, but was written in the 1950's, and was now in our hands at the exact moment was quite astounding. We were speaking on the phone trying to share the discovery of this amazing historical account of Black Elk's dreams and visions of what was to come of the world. The coincidence of all of this happening at the same time was not lost on either of us. We were in sync with each other and found that Black Elk certainly did have much to say, and that he intended both of us to 'hear it.'

I include this synopsis on the importance of our dreams: "This chapter makes me consider the insistent importance of our dreams and our rituals. Perhaps we should be paying much more attention to our dreams and to the powers given to us through them as well as to the rituals of prayer, meditation, Eucharist, etc. by which we activate the healing powers endowed to us in our dreams. If we continue to ignore these gifts, we might risk spiritual and even physical danger. If we attend to these gifts, our vision and understanding might change so that those things which we once thought to be dangerous and threatening might become loving and generous, like a relative, or even like an angel."

Black Elk Speaks Chapter 14: 'The Horse Dance' a posted review by Deforest London December 14, 2016.

Peeling Energy

The Lesson of Layers

I had a dream experience of my mother shortly after her passing, I was still raw from the loss, but also from my persistent replay of the decisions made on her behalf during her illness. I relived every opportunity and choice until I was satisfied that all had been carefully weighed, and that I had done my best in every action and charge. I was satisfied with my behavior, and then I gave it all back to God.

I had not yet dozed off, when I heard the words, "You are still serving her" What? I thought, now completely lucid and awake, but not understanding the meaning of the words, I lay there thinking of them and what they could possibly mean, and soon fell into sleep. I had a dream clearly marked as a metaphor and a lesson called THE DREAM OF LAYERS.

I dreamed of my mother living in a big house in the hills of California. She was still my mother, but a different kind of person than the mother I had known. She was a more-worldly version of herself, wearing lots of jewelry and fine clothing that seemed completely out of her character. Her personality was so different. She was demanding and bossy, and she ordered my brothers about, and they were quick to respond to her wishes, and that was also different.

She was moving, and I was in full Realtor mode questioning what stays and what goes. I saw a pile of beautiful room size rugs stacked on top of one another, they were at least 4 or 5 deep as I counted and rolled up the corners to reveal a different pattern and color. I looked at the difference in each one, until I asked her, "Mom, what is all of this? These should all be removed," and as I got to the bottom of the pile, a beautiful solid wood floor was exposed. She answered that she had wanted to 'PROTECT THE ORIGINAL FLOOR.'

At the exact moment she said this, I was given a knowing that this dream was a continuation of another dream I had several years ago about the many different dimensions when our lives are paused at the crossroads of life changing decisions.

I was shown twelve rotating bubbles circling in front of me, and I was asked to make a movement, and so I stuck out my tongue, or flash a big smile, and this action would be captured within the bubble and then it would float away. This was a representation of a new version of my life within the bubble floating off to be lived in another dimension. (see full dream in volume one 'GIFTS FROM THE EDGE Stories of the Other Side', lesson titled Cause and Effect)

When one action is taken, and the other road is not traveled, so to speak, is really being played out somewhere else. It has taken on a life of its own. An example is of a divorce, a huge crossroad in one's life. What I was shown was that the new life of choice was created, and you are living it, but the older version, still married, is being played out, and you are still together in another dimension.

It was a huge concept for me, and I don't profess to completely understand it, but I was in spirit school when given this example. As I considered this concept, and put it into words that I could reverb back to the teacher, "that there must be so many lives being played out in so many different dimensions," the teacher actually turned and clapped, and announced to the class, that this one (me) gets an A.

Anyway, back on track of this dream of my mother...

I was then shown three representations of my mother's lives:

a. My life now, with my mother deceased.
b. My mother still ill, a few different decisions had kept her alive, but she was tragically ill, and she was suffering. I was still at her side, still serving her, and trying my best to keep her alive.
c. The turn of events in her life, money, lots of it, finer things, bigger homes, she had changed into a much harder version

of herself, toughened by life and material wealth. I still loved her, but stepping into this life, was all so very different.

I realized that I was shown examples of the many dimensions and lives she and I share together, and that they are playing themselves out 'somewhere else.'

I had been shown this lesson before, but now with the use of my mother as an aide, it really brought the point home to me.

There was also a new element shared within this example, and I am still trying to process it, but I will add it here because it is important:

We come to this life to learn, achieve, test. We come in whole, with the amount of energy needed to sustain us for the trip, but as we grow and come to life's crossroads, a part of our energy is 'PEELED OFF' this was the word that was given to me to help me understand the process.

The peeling off of energy accompanies the sphere or bubble as it goes off in another direction. As it bubbles off, it takes a bit of our original energy with it, to sustain it. This diminishes the whole, or the original energy.

There is plenty of it to start with, we are young and we play and run. But as our lives progress, and we begin 'branching out' and facing different decisions and crossroads, more and more of our original energy is depleted. Eventually this leaves us a bit older and more tired. This is normal here (on Earth) as aging is inevitable, so it is not entirely the energy sharing that makes us old, but it does contribute to our weariness.

Note: this next paragraph is SPECULATORY on my part.

As we have less of ourselves in our original state, I am left to wonder, if you are a worrier or anxious about your decisions, or perhaps have had more life experiences or loves, would it not hasten this dissipation? Again, this question is purely speculation on my part, and has not been confirmed, but I continue... because I have not been asked to stop... have they peeled off so much of themselves that they have little energy left? And can there be too many lives peeled off from the original?

I will expand on this if I receive more, but I am sure of the lesson as I was shown, and that the 'peeling off' of our energy to support other versions of ourselves is very real.

Expecting to Fly

As a dear friend and proud grandmother, Charlene often shares pictures and stories of her three-year-old granddaughter Roxy. She is a dark haired, blue-eyed beauty with a quick wit and a happy smile that can light up the world. She has won all of our hearts, but sadly she lives an ocean away from the grandmother she loves and adores.

They have a close bond between them, sharing frequent phone calls, and Roxy loves watching for the cherished boxes sent her way. They are filled with handmade dresses, that Roxy loves showing her friends and cousins. There is a special tag sewn in the back of each one that reads 'MADE BY GRANDMA' and because the fabric and style is chosen especially for Roxy, they are always the ones she chooses to wear. "Grandmas dresses please" and she will twirl and spin around in them, knowing she is especially loved.

During this morning's phone visit, Roxy couldn't wait to tell her of the 'special dream' she had the night before. In her very best three-year-old language she described how she and Grandma had played together, and Charlene indulged her by replying, "well that sounds fun honey, what were we doing?" and Roxy told her that they had played tag and games of hide and seek.

Wanting to keep the conversation rolling, Charlene asked her how she got to her house, and Roxy confidently answered, "I flew," "Oh did you fly on a big airplane?" Charlene asked, "no grandma" was her quick retort, and then the tone in her voice changed, and she spoke more clearly and slowly, stretching the words out to give them more emphases, "I... F L E W..."

Charlene was perplexed, and asked her again, wanting to clarify, "you flew, but not on an airplane?" "Yes grandma" she said, and with her best teaching voice Roxy explained,

> *"If you put your arms out like this when you go to sleep,*
> *you can fly anywhere you want."*

This statement was filled with so much more than childlike wonder and innocence. Because there was such a certainty in her words, it made Charlene hold her breath. And then in her own serious voice, she asked, "Will you come and visit me again soon Roxy?" and with that, she could feel her little granddaughters love carried though all of the miles that separated them, "Yes grandma, I promise, I'll come again real soon."

4

The Astral Plane

"Not alive on Earth, nor dwelling in the light of Heaven."

What Is the Astral Plane?

I feel a prompting to write about the Astral Plane, and the choice of a world-like place to dwell after earth life is over. It is NOT HEAVEN AND NOT HELL, but a place for the deceased who are not yet ready to let go of Earth. It is the closest thing to it, and those who live there are in a kind of holding pattern, some not even realizing they are dead, this is the dimension one would say a ghost comes from.

I see and hear these souls from time to time, and it took some practice in the early years of discovering my abilities, to discern the differences of communication. Although the souls of the Astral Plane have a higher vibration than the living, it is not on a level of higher consciousness, and for me it has a distinct feeling that comes with it: not scary, but with a bit of a darker teasing tone to it.

They seem joyful in having found someone who can 'hear' them and find it funny to interject tidbits including numbers or names. I have spent a lot of time trying to look them up, having had little luck on the internet and Google. I think that the message they give is more in recognition, and a bookmark of their life. They were here, they were real and on Earth with a name and an actual existence, and they would like to be remembered.

The souls in the Astral Plane are the same as they were here, and their personality carries the same emotional baggage. If they were sad, addicted, jealous, mad, while on the Earth and choose not to fully cross over when they die, they don't have the opportunity to view their life from the 360-degree review. They have not had a chance to learn from their experience, or even recognize that it was a lesson they had asked for. They have not met with the elders, or their guides, and have not listened to their own hearts. They are just mad or lost in the outcome.

I have never encountered one that would harm me, though a few have managed to appear way too close in my visual screen. Their faces will suddenly appear, jumping in or towards me in an attempt to frighten. In one instance, a young woman wore wild tussled hair and googly eyed goggles that had actual springs attached to the lenses, so when she suddenly popped so close into my view, they sprang out like a slinky toy or an ad in a kid's magic/gadget magazine. She got the attention she was trying to achieve, and it is more funny than scary now that I have made the choice not to let fear rule over me.

I have read of many who can communicate with, and assist them in finding the light, though I have found that this is not my calling. Very rarely do I have both visual and audio at the same time. I have waved them off like a bothersome gnat when I am tired, adding a slightly snarky "go to the light" when irritated by their persistence.

Lucy

One encounter did make it through using both visual and audio. At first, I just saw her face, it is usually like a very detailed chalk drawing on a black background. I blinked her away, but then thought, there must be a reason she has come to me. I called out to her to come back, and I asked if I could help her. She answered me with a quick "No!"

I asked for her name, and she paused before answering in a little softer tone, "Lucy."

I asked her if she could see the light, and I said it was there somewhere if she would just look for it, but she was not interested in finding it.

I asked her what had happened to her, and why she chose to remain there, and she answered me in a kind of broken chuckle:

"One Thousand Reasons,

One Thousand Cracks"

I am not sure if it was me who lost the connection, or if she just chose to leave knowing there was not much I could do for her. But I did notice that there seemed to be both an accountability, and a bit of victimhood in her choice of words.

I have thought of her from time to time, in hopes that Lucy has found her way to the light, but it is up to her because she still has free will. She is exercising that will, to stay where she is, and to remain comfortably lost in the Astral Plane. She is not being punished, or damned to hell, but I am made to understand that sometimes one will choose to punish themselves, and they have the gift of free will to do it.

The Special Bus

I know when it is time to ground myself again, or when I have left myself vulnerable to the mischievous ones. I visualize being surrounded by light, and I use the imagery of being wrapped in a protective bubble to keep them at bay. On the other hand, I have also found that when I am too protected, it can hinder my gift, and can limit my openness to the Heaven Connection. I do not want to lose the opportunity of communication with my loved ones, Spirit School, or the nudges of my guides. It is a fine line to travel indeed.

I have spoken before of the Earth's ascension process that is taking place. There is much work being done on our behalf, beyond the veil. Negative energy is being released from the earth, it is the stress and tension we have felt growing stronger lately. It must be released to flow back to God to be cleansed and remodeled. All is of a natural order and balance, and room must be made for the new energy of love and acceptance. As positivity and light come to help us, more of the negative energy must be given back to be healed. Balance is key.

I asked my guide about this healing process, and if this affects the Astral Plane as well. The answer came that night in a profound dream of a bus. It was an ordinary everyday yellow school bus, full of souls looking out from each window. Each was an individual of a different age, size, gender and race.

The bus had stopped, and the door stood opened, but they sat perfectly still as they looked out to their new location with curiosity and worry. A guide in a cream-colored robe would take their hand, and lovingly lead them down the steps of the bus. The troubled newcomers were receiving one-on-one assistance to acclimate to their new surroundings.

They needed to be moved because the Astral Plane is also being cleansed of the negative energy it holds. The guiding helper's assignment is an important part of the process, because these souls are not to be left behind, as none will be left behind. Instead they are given loving guidance from an advanced volunteer.

I think there were two reasons I was granted this visual. The first being an answer to a concise question about where these souls had gone, and the second, was the understanding that came with the visual. The sister I had lost many years ago, was now in training to be one of these loving guides. She would play a pivotal role in the Earth's transition into the 5th dimension. Souls in the astral plane are in the process of being transported to a safe location, in another 3-dimensional world. I saw that my angel sister was one of these loving guides, and she was learning how to be a helper in this important work.

I went outside to sit and enjoy the warm morning air after this dream. I was recording it in my dream journal, and I was thinking of my sister. She was always so sweet and kind, and so angelic in her actions, this was the perfect job for her as she was always so willing to help. 'She will do well' I thought, and I felt a sense of pride in all she has accomplished, in this life, and now in the next.

It had been some time since I had spoken with her, funny how life moves on, the lost feeling of not being able to phone her anymore, was replaced by my ability to reach her in the beyond. Yet even in this miracle of communication, there had been a gradual slowing down, perhaps I had finally gotten used to her passing.

Wondering if we were still as strongly connected, I called out to her "Kay, we haven't talked in a while, Kay, are you still there? I am wondering if I can still hear you? Kay can you still hear me?"

I didn't have to wait too long for her answer, "I'm here whenever you need me to be." I found such relief in making this connection again, "Kay, I was wondering about my dream last night, are you in training as a guide as I was being shown?" She answered, "you are on the right track, so to speak."

I explained what I was shown, that she was a guide calming confused souls that were being transported to a new location, 'the right track', I thought, and I heard her giggle, and repeat the words "right track"

"Thank You, Thank You for still coming to me" I said, and she answered "I am always with you, always" and with that confirmation I started to say goodbye to her but stopped short, "I wanted to ask you one more thing, is there anything you have for me, to guide or share?" She responded with one-word, *"PURSUE..."* and then she said it again, slowly and deliberately *"Per---sue"* and she laughed as I repeated it with a questioning tone, "Pursue what? More reading and studying, what more am I supposed to do to pursue?" and she answered me, "you're on track" and I repeated on track...on track, in my head until I remembered her saying earlier 'the right track', haha, I made a funny back at her, "yes, she said, "the right track" and with that she was gone.

I decided to look up 'Pursue' in the dictionary, and here is the definition that stuck out and made me laugh: "continue or proceed along (a path or route)." I chuckled as it aligned with what she had said earlier, "on track."

I was 'on track', and the bus was on 'the right track', and my question of her new job was also on 'the right track.'

It was wonderful to affirm our connection; we were still in tune with one another enough to share sister sillies. I love you Kaylyn, good luck on your new pursuit: (the action of following or pursuing someone or something.)

Double Pane

I woke this morning feeling so very safe and secure.

I saw myself in a dream, standing beside a huge picture window. I could see many Zombie-like creatures outside, they were a type of living dead. They snarled and waved their arms as they moved towards me, but they were being held back by the window that stood between us. It was unlike a regular window, but was specially constructed to protect me and keep them at bay.

I was shown that it was possible for me to ignore those of the Astral Plane who would choose to disrupt my life. Although I could still see and hear them if I chose to, I would be protected from any harm they could cause me. I was shown that although I couldn't 'see' the protection, it was there, and I could trust in its strength to keep me from harm.

I have chosen to ignore those who try to reach me from their dark state of confusion and anger over their own situation and existence in the Astral Plane. This state is of their own choosing, and they must learn to look for the light in order to leave this dimension.

I am a target so to speak, because of my ability to see and hear them, but no longer will I fear them. I am finally free, knowing I am protected, and feel only gratitude for my guides and angels who protect me from the 'troubled dead' as I work towards communicating with the light on Other Side.

THANK YOU GOD, for the double pane of protection.

What you're thinking is what you're becoming.

- Muhammad Ali

5

The Seeker

"What Does 'Awakening' Mean?"

The following quote from Ellyn Dye, seemed a spot-on answer, she is a wonderful teacher, NDE experiencer, keynote speaker and friend.

"An Awakening is a sudden shift in perspective and understanding about Who We Really Are. It can include a new understanding of "God" and our place in the Universe—and the place of others, such as the understanding that we are all One (interconnected and ultimately from the same Source, with the same spark of the Divine inside)." © Ellyn Dye, *Tunnel Vision Newsletter,* Spring 2019 (LionMagic.com)

Soul to Soul

In this time of the public demonstrations that profile our worldly divisions of race, color, political and gender preference, a picture came up in a Facebook post of two human skeletons. Underneath the picture, a question was posed, which one was black, and which one was transgender? Profound questions I thought since we all do look the same underneath our skin.

We are so much more than the vehicle our soul inhibits. Although it a miraculous work of breath and heartbeat, it is by definition a meat suit we wear to experience Earth, the physical learning/playing field gifted to us by a loving God.

Underneath the embodiment of muscle and bone, we are a magnificent and beautiful essence, a forever living energy created by Source, the creator of all things. We are our souls, and everything that our soul has experienced and learned is what we get to take back with us after we have used the body up, and it dies and is left behind.

Before our birth, we accepted the contract to come here under a veil of forgetfulness. If we were to remember our own grandeur, we could never truly be tested by hardships imposed on us by our own design and plan.

We accepted the mission and created contracts with others to assist us by playing vital roles during this marvelous expedition. We came in with veiled memories of the splendor of our true home and with a subconscious list of to-dos, that we have no recall or memory of.

No wonder we have an innermost feeling of loneliness, and questions that we just cannot explain.

I am focused on my personal training of being mindful and working to look past the outer-ness of color, gender, stature, hair and clothing, the things my eyes see, and to look beyond the skin of those I meet, and know. I often ask myself, what is their story, their mission here, and how do I fit into that mission, and what am I to learn from this person, and what does that person need to learn from me?

I had a wonderful incident about ten years ago as I became aware or awake as others have termed it. The time when you become cognizant of the spiritual nature of all around you and you work with an intent to incorporate it more fully into your life.

For the Briefest of Moments

I had just come out of a fast food restaurant, fumbling with my keys and the paper bag. As I walked toward my car, I noticed a young black man on the sidewalk in front of me looking down at his phone. For some reason he looked up at me, not so unusual you might say, but as a chunky silver haired woman well over sixty, you get used to a sort of invisibility by the young. If you are over fifty you know exactly what I'm talking about here.

As I approached, he lifted his head from his phone and turned to look directly into my eyes, and the biggest of smiles shot across his face. It was warm and inviting, and it seemed as if time had slowed down enough for me to take note. A flash of insight hit me as I looked at his face. I realized that I was not just seeing his face, but that this was a soul to soul moment, and I was seeing into who he truly was, and he was seeing me, the real me, and I grinned right back at him.

Although it lasted only a brief moment in time, it had a distinct feeling attached to it, and I knew that I would never forget it. We had connected with a type of hello that went beyond the physical of our bodies. Our souls knew each other, remembered each other, and it warmed me to my core. We had communicated, soul wise.

In the smallest of moments, we had looked beyond skin and age. It was fleeting, and time would soon catch up. In a flash he realized his gesture was out of place and he quickly retracted it, looking immediately back at his phone and letting me pass without further recognition.

There were no words to be spoken as none were needed. All had been said without a sound, but I cherish this experience, and my participation in a real soul to soul contact, and the invitation to look beyond all that would seem to make us incompatible strangers.

Hey, Has Anyone Got a Key?

In the early years of my spiritual awakening, I had a great visual while meditating, and I learned that indeed, there is purpose in the timing of our progression.

A young man stood alone amongst a sea of parked cars. He seemed to be distressed and moving his head about as if he were looking for, and eventually finding his own car. He proceeded to climb on its roof, and yell, *"Hey, has anyone got a key?"*

The vision of the young man has stayed with me as I thought about the greater meaning and personal interpretation that it held. It finally dawned on me that as I advance into a deeper awareness and spiritual enlightenment, that I will often read, or be witness to someone else's beautiful gift of communication and can feel a twinge of envy. I am not speaking jealousy in a malicious way, but rather an inquisitive wondering of the whys. Why aren't my dreams as vivid, or why don't I feel a closer connection, or why can't I auto write or channel an arch angel? You know, it's the equivalent of why he and not me, because they appeared to have found their way, and I sincerely wanted to find mine.

This visual really sparked something within me. Because I have poured through all forms of spiritual literature, NDE stories, and joined countless Facebook groups comprised of other seekers for so many years. I was looking for something that seemed just beyond my reach. I knew the answers to my questions were out there, I just couldn't find them.

There were many times that I felt frustrated, even as the answers began to formulate within me, and I asked for more, wanting it all to come faster. This frustration would show itself in my dreams, as I would walk down a hallway of many locked doors.

In one dream I stood in front of one of these doors, knowing instinctively that this entrance was mine to open. I began to knock on it until a voice interrupted me and asked, *"Why do you not use your own key to unlock the door?"* I was ready to retort that I didn't have a key, but before I spoke, I realized that I was wearing a small satchel on my left wrist, and was suddenly aware that indeed, I carried my own key.

It came to me that this young man was asking to use someone else's key to start HIS own cars engine, and that just won't work. Each key is individualized for each particular and unique car, and another's key will not fit.

This metaphor is much like looking for someone else to provide an open door into spiritual advancement, but each of us has our own path and our own time frame, built with our own learning curves.

We carry our own key within us, it may feel misplaced at times but it is not lost, and it is up to us to find it and start our own engine.

Now, as I reflect on the visual of the young man atop his vehicle asking if anyone has a key, it all made sense. The sea of cars around him were everyone's individual way to move toward knowledge, and everyone has their own door to open, and no one else's key will unlock another's door towards enlightenment.

Find and treasure your own key, dear reader, because you must have it to start your own individual journey.

Wow... Did I Get Read

My Spirit Guide, apparently wasn't very happy with me as I tried to find a medium to help my daughter in law Jami, connect to her mother on the Other Side. I was lying in bed trying to come up with a plan of who to call, someone who I knew to be talented and yet, someone I could afford.

The following words came to me:

"Why do you not use your own gifts?
You have a key, yet you continually wait for the door to open.
Is it the exchange of money that would make another's gift more real?
Do you not have the capability to do as any other who sees?
Are you not the one to accomplish this?
Why do you wait for the door to open as you hold the key?
Use it. Go in and get what you want"

I understood that I had just been read by my guide, because I had not considered myself as the answer to my own needs. I had received so much and yet I was still timid and unsure of my own gifts. I reacted, and went right to work, unwrapping a wonderful gift of intuition and the ability to reach my loved ones who reside beyond the stars.

I thank my guide for the wakeup call and the swift kick in the backside, and also for showing me the door. I could hear the knocking, but I had not yet opened it, not until he helped me notice that I carried my own key, and that I'd had it all along. It was hanging from my wrist in a satin satchel, I didn't need anyone to open the door for me, it was mine to unlock all along.

An Old Friend Drops In

Every once and awhile, I dream of a friend, a soul friend, and the someone I have known for eons and eons of time. For whatever reason she is not on Earth now, I am here without her, but she comes to me in dreams, dropping in for a quick visit every once and awhile just to say hello.

One evening I dreamed of us playing together as young children, I can still see the dark hair that flowed at her side, though I have no memory of her face. My attention was on the ball that we passed back and forth as we played and conversed. It shined brightly from the inside out, a brilliant light coming from within it, as if we were passing a star between us.

When she leaves I am filled with the warmth and the memory of a trusted connection I have with her. She is a true friend with an unbroken bond of support, and a knowing that she waits for me to come back home again.

One weekend with my husband out of town, I filled the bed with pillows, and spread my favorite books all around me. The bedside table held drinks and snacks, all had been set up for the evening ahead, as I was having a personal pajama party in his absence.

After hours of reading, I began to get sleepy and fell softly into the relaxed state of theta, (see sleep cycle charts) it is the whimsical state between wakefulness and sleep. It was in this state, that I noticed someone else was with me, but I was not afraid, my friend was coming to join the party.

She was wearing her pajamas too, and in this situation of comfortable familiarity, I remembered her. It was my friend who had come to join me now in this personal party mode, and nothing seemed unusual or out of the ordinary. I accepted her entrance as commonplace, as if we had shared many bestie sleepovers in the past.

She was in a sitting position, her long legs stretched out straight, and she was floating downward into the scene in my room. The floating was slow and exaggerated, as if a point was being made, that she was coming DOWN, but the feeling was not coming down from heaven, but rather from the sky, she was coming from the stars.

I focused my attention on her face, though I did not recognize it, her features were so different from mine. Her hair was pulled back into a tight ponytail, exposing a chiseled jawline, large cheek bones and slanted dark eyes, and her limbs and fingers were exceptionally long. She looked very much like the girl in the Avatar movie, except that her skin was not blue.

We shared bouts of laughter throughout the evening, and when it was over, and the scene began to fade, I asked aloud for her to wait, "please wait", and I asked for her name. I heard her reply, something like Marium, Maryum, no, that's not quite right, it was more like mirror, Mirrorum, Mirry'um and with that, all disappeared from my sight.

After waking up, I lay in the dark with so many questions, and I began to ask for some clarification from my guide. As I began to speak, I got a large bright flash in my right eye, like a star or quasar that becomes brilliant just before it goes out, and I felt I had received a sign that I was on the right track, and to continue with my questions.

Perhaps there is truth in what several mediums have told me, that I am from the stars?

Could it be that Earth is not the only world I have lived on? Years earlier, I met an amazing woman in Colorado who had studied as a shaman, and when she met me, she told me outright, that I was of Star origin, and yet was deeply grounded in the Earth. She told me this made me different and rare. The information seemed far beyond my comprehension at the time, but I thanked her for it, and I captured her words in my journal. Now, days after the visit/experience, while putting my books away, I opened the journal by happenstance, and the words seemed to pop from the page, was I being shown another wonderful piece of the spiritual puzzle?

Could this really be a friend that I left behind while I came here to experience earth?

"Was she waiting for me to return home for good after my earth lessons?"

"Did I originally look like her?"

"And is this my true identity?"

The experience left me with many more questions, than answers. And yet, I am left with a confident assurance that I have a wonderful friend waiting for me, in a next life somewhere, on the Other Side, or perhaps even in the stars beyond. In a way, it does not really matter where she waits, it is enough for now to know of her, and that she is waiting for me, and I will leave an opening in my mind to ponder and learn more if allowed.

What I know for sure is that there is so much that I do not know for sure.

Until then, I will hold onto this memory, kindling the bouts of laughter and joy we were able to share in our lovely visit together, confident within the knowing that I have a treasured friend out there somewhere, in the great beyond.

I Would Love Them

On January 30, 2015, I had a beautiful dream experience, waking to remember that I was standing on a stage as a guest speaker of some type. I have no recall of the what or the why, or even who my audience was, but at one point a large screen appeared on stage with me, and I saw that it contained at least twenty pictures in single stacked frames.

The pictures were close-up facial photos of everyday people. There were men, some were bearded, and some were bald. Included were women with curly hair and some with full red lips. Some were younger with tight muscles and bright eyes, and some were very old. There were children's faces included in the picture box, some wearing glasses, or hats, and each person's skin was a different color, black, white, red, yellow and brown.

As the audience and I studied the photos, a question was asked of me, "How would you help them?" I thought for a moment before I approached the screen, raising my hand and cupping the chin of one portrayed in a photo, and I answered with sincere intent:

"I WOULD LOVE THEM."

I have thought of this moment on a world stage for almost five years now, and I have done my best to live up to my answer, and I hold myself accountable for my own words.

The Universal Outreach

There is a universal outreach of guides, helpers and angels, just waiting to help us on our journey here. They stand at the ready to answer our questions, and if you don't feel that you have been heard, perhaps you need to adjust the way you ask your questions.

I came up with a formula that helps me obtain answers, and it's quite elementary really. I ask my question, and I offer my guide an easy way to answer. If the answer is yes, I ask to see it as YES, or a number 1, ONE. If the answer is no, I ask to see NO or number 2, TWO.

The seeing of these numbers is to happen within a dream, because after years of practicing lucid dreaming, this is my most trusted place to experience spiritual direction. I am careful not to manipulate the answer to my questions, and so my answers must be clearly stated on a billboard or road sign etc. so there is no confusion of the answer, or where it came from.

Are all of my questions answered? No, they are not, especially in the beginning of my awakening and adaptation of this technique. I would wake and realize there had been no answer given, and sadly, I would often accept a null outcome as the answer. That is until my guide gave me a proverbial kick in the butt one night and spoke directly into my dream:

"IF YOU ARE NOT GETTING ANSWERS TO YOUR QUESTIONS, ASK BETTER QUESTIONS."

I realized that my simple formula would not work when I asked a muddled or unanswerable question, and I had to practice being precise in what I asked, and also in the reason I was asking the question in the first place.

A good example of this came from a like-minded friend, as she related a story of her mother's daily prayers and requests for an easier life. She was serious about it, asking for this every day and night. She was tired of her job, bills, mortgage and car payments, and just wanted a break from it all. She would often announce that she just wanted to stay home and watch TV.

She prayed earnestly to become debt free and to live a simple, worry free life, and one day her prayers were answered, and she finally got exactly what she asked for in the way of a serious car accident.

The car was totaled, and there were no more payments required now, it was gone. She was seriously hurt, her arm and elbow broken in many places and in between operations, so much time was spent convalescing in front of the TV, she subsequently lost her job. This left her no way to make any of her payments, and eventually she lost her home to bankruptcy and foreclosure. She was all but homeless until she eventually found a modest cabin on the outskirts of town. She had a much simpler life now, and all of her requests had been answered, but she laughed as she told the story, realizing that she learned that she would be more specific in the future, perhaps just praying to win the lottery next time.

There are times in my dreams that I receive a number 3, THREE for an answer, this is definitely a note from my guide and friend I call Click Click. He has a wonderful sense of humor and this is his way of getting my attention and telling me that there is not a way for him to answer the question as stated, and I need to start over and ask a better question.

Truman's World

So many of the stories I write about come from my dreams, I capture them in the journals that I keep near my bedside. When I wrote my first book, 'GIFTS FROM THE EDGE, Stories of the Other Side', I fingered through the bookshelf full of the journals that collected many years of miraculous and vivid dreams, and I let them speak for themselves. The ones that were included would stand out from the page, and I would revisit stories that were on my mind when I woke.

When it became clear to me that I was to write another book, I was soaking in the tub in an oasis of hot water and bubbles. It came to me as a flash of insight, another book? "Really", I questioned, because the first one was so hard to bring to completion. Not in the writing of it, as the stories seemed to pour onto the page, but going through the publishing process is not for the faint of heart or the shallow of pocket.

I began throwing every excuse not to do it again into the air around me, but stopped short when I had vision, and saw the book as almost finished. The stories were written and gathered in a large binder, complete with a picture of the front cover, this image was given to me, along with the title, 'LESSONS FROM THE OTHER SIDE.'

In the vision I saw myself seated at a small table with two chairs, and there was someone seated across from me, a woman, someone I knew from the beyond, and I felt her as the *'Divine Feminine'*, though I do not remember her name. I clearly saw myself present the binder, the cover and titles facing her directly as I gently pushed it towards her using both hands. There was ceremony in this presentation, and the respect I held for her was beyond words, she had asked me to do this, insomuch as telling me that I was Worthy to do this, and all of my excuses not to do it evaporated.

    I got into bed energized, and ready to do my part, to sleep and dream and receive. I lay there in a comfortable position, and waited, and waited. I was expecting something instantaneous, like someone to 'drop' some knowledge on me. I waited there for quite a while, all revved up and ready for what seemed like hours, until I heard the chuckle, ahh, my guide. He comes into my head not exactly what I will call as audible, but I can hear him, and his sense of humor usually precedes him. I thought what's so funny now? And his reply was that I had enough material in my journals already, and I needed to go back through them, and I would find what was needed for the book. Anything else that was to be included would come to me, but only after I had done the work. I added the following story as one of the inspirations I received, after doing the work.

    My husband and I took a quick vacation in MOAB Utah, spending days along the trails and beautiful cliff lines. We were staying in a cabin along the Colorado river, but the weather was so cold and rainy, I did little else but park myself in front of the fireplace and write while in the solace of the red dirt mountains and slick rocks.

    One evening before retiring we turned on the TV. There were only a few stations available in the cabin, and we had a choice of the 24-hour news, a game show, cartoons, or a movie that had just started playing. It was called 'The Truman Show' and it had an interesting plot line about watching a young man since birth in a completely controlled environment. Everything and everyone he knew, including his own wife and mother were paid actors participating in this live experiment staring Jim Carrey.

His life was on display for television viewers 24 hours a day, every day. The nation was so intrigued by his simple unawareness of the real world the rest of us lived in. He only knew his world, where day and night and even the weather was inspired by a button on a control panel.

The movie was wrapped within the theme of a young man who began to feel that there just had to be more to life than the predictable day to day routine happening in the small town he now felt trapped in. He began to dream of exploration and travel, as something within him arose and grew stronger. All efforts were made by the cast and crew to squelch his curiosity and to keep him put in his perfectly safe box of a world.

At one point the show's creator/producer gave an interview to the viewing audience and was asked the question, "Why do you think Truman never came close to discovering the true nature of his world until now?" The producer answered, "Because we accept the reality of the world with which we are presented, it is as simple as that."

I write now of your own opportunity to be a seeker, you do not have to simply accept the reality you were given, open yourself up to some new ideas of the life-after-life, and the reasons why you are here. You don't have to keep anything that does not feel right to you, use your instincts as they are one of your greatest tools of discernment.

In closing, I want to share the words I heard one morning as I drifted into wakefulness:

"ANSWERS ARE MEANINGLESS TO SOMEONE WHO IS NOT ASKING QUESTIONS."

I offer, that it is OK to ask questions and to challenge your beliefs. Question yourself, are they truly YOUR beliefs, or like Truman, have you just accepted the reality of the world as it was presented to you?

6

Who Are you, Really?

Discoveries Within

*"When you've made a decision of who someone is,
You remove the opportunity for them to be anything else."*

- Claudia Watts Edge

A Very Special Visit

I am having trouble finding words to describe the following dream/experience. Sacred comes to mind, as the experience is delicate and special beyond my ability to describe it.

In my dream, I was told that 'someone' wanted to speak to me, and the arrangements were almost complete. Their name was either not given, or veiled from my memory, but she was majestic and regal, and someone I looked up to with love and admiration in the spirit world, and she was coming to speak with me.

I was honored and humbled as I approached the box that she had arrived in. It was built as a form of protection while visiting Earth, as she was so pure in thought and heart she could not be exposed to any of Earth's negativity and darkness.

There were windows in the box, and as I approached I could see inside to the décor of living greenery with flowers and tropical birds, it was more than a constructed box, it was alive and radiated light from within itself.

I saw her face from the side before she turned to me and offered her hand, and I recognized her instantly in my heart, as someone that I knew from the beyond.

She was exquisite, poised and grand, and yet her simple dress of cream-colored muslin, covered all but her face and hands. Her head was covered in the same cloth, her hair only partially exposed, but I could see it was long and dark.

Oh God, it was all so very beautiful, and it is almost impossible to describe the feeling of love that I was exposed to while there. Love and Light just radiated from within her and I was bathed in it, even before she motioned me to take a seat at the small table across from her.

I hold on to the dearest memory of her face, her skin was like light, with a glow of white and gold that came deep from within it. It filled and illuminated the entirety of her countenance. I marveled at her beauty, her dark eyes and slim nose, and her lips carried a tone of the softest red, but it was not an applied color, it was a natural hue that was hers alone, and I was completely captivated in the poetic ease and simplicity of her beauty.

The honor of it all, did not escape me. She cared so very much for me and I felt it to my very core. I was completely humbled and yet she did not make me feel that she was my superior, and I was made to know that we were to have a two-sided conversation, as equals.

She could not have been more gracious, or more loving towards me, and we laughed together like old friends.

I do not know how long I was with her, or all of what was said, nor do I remember our goodbyes, but I woke knowing that I am deeply cared for, and grateful for being allowed to remember the experience.

There was one thing she said that I was able to keep with me, and it came to mind as I lay in the darkness recalling the splendor of it all while the tears rolled down my cheeks. This magnificent someone was telling me that I WAS WORTHY, and that I could do it, and that I was WORTHY to do it. Whatever it is I am supposed to do, I know I will do it especially for her simply because she has asked me to. I did not recall her name, or if one was even given, but the words 'Divine Feminine' came to mind as I scoured my memory for it.

The room was still dark as I made my way to the bath and filled the tub with warm sudsy water. I did not want to sleep, and I could not control my tears, something remarkable had happened, and I wanted to hold onto the experience for as long as I could. I savored the beauty of it, and I held myself while recanting the feeling of the love that poured out from her and into me.

"I Am Worthy to do this" I thought aloud, "to do what?"

In those moments I felt a download of information come into me, as if it was being showered from overhead. I was to write a second book, this book, and I was even given the title, LESSONS FROM THE OTHER SIDE, and I had a clear understanding of what the chapters would contain. It was all but laid out for me.

I fought the urge to say no, or hell no as I wanted to, because the first book had been such a test of my resolve to get it into publication.

Anyone who has ever written a book exposing the very core of who they are, and going through the process of self-publishing, will understand the sacrifices. There is also the use of their own money, and for me, what could be drawn from a limited budget, while their partner complains of the time that is being devoted to this 'hobby' saying that it is marginalizing what could be done for the family.

My creative need to birth it into fruition while facing direct opposition and inconceivable roadblocks, even included an accident that cut deeply into the meat of my right hand. It required many stitches and a resulting need to type half of the book in a hunt and peck style using the non-dominate left. I was driven to prove to myself that I could and would finish it, no matter what the obstacles, and so I did.

I want to put to rest any thoughts that a spiritual writer does any of this in hopes of making money or even a living. We pray all of the way through for help in surviving the process as we pull from the gut what we feel is supposed to be shared. There is also a willingness to give up the safety of anonymity, while considering that our family and friends may find us odd, or even being pushed away. There is a strange lonesome in this work of being a hand maiden or soldier for God.

All of this went through my mind as I remembered what I was in for by agreeing to do it all over again. How would I explain this to my husband? But there was no way I would even consider saying no to 'HER,' of course I would do it.

May I offer that I am not claiming this book to be a new world wonder in any way, my hopes are simply that it is able to reach the people who were meant to receive the information within. The joy of accomplishment is the payment for this labor of love, and I do it for both 'her' and you dear reader, but especially for myself as I test my own resolve and my willingness to do it.

You are worthy, too.

Walk with Me

The walls in my office are covered with framed photos of family, my children and my grandchildren in action. I love to take a moment in a busy day to tilt back in my chair and look at the familiar faces of the ones I love.

There is another picture that I have placed amongst them, and it too has a familiar face.

It is a picture I took from my mother's bedroom after she passed, and its feeling of familiarity stems from the many years it rested near her bedside table. When I look at it, even now, it makes me feel close to her.

It is painted with an illuminating light technique, and in a Thomas Kinkade kind of style and rendition. It is a depiction of the bible story of Jesus and the young woman at the water well. I am not a bible scholar, but I did grow up with the stories of Jesus in Sunday School, and I continue to have a sincere love for him and his teachings, though I do not consider myself religious.

For me the picture depicts an approachable Jesus, sitting comfortably on the stones at the edge of the well. He is listening to a young woman who sits in a kind of half kneeling/sitting position at his feet. The conversation they are having is an example of the dreams I have with headlines stating they are story metaphors, and the teachings are easier to re-tell using symbolism.

This picture speaks a thousand words to me, because he is so very present in their conversation, and he is really listening to her. A man with good communication skills, now that's enough reason to love him right there.

This is how I would picture myself if I ever had a chance to meet him, kneeling in a show of respect of his sacrifices and teachings. I have said more than once that I long to touch the hem of his garment. This statement offers a depiction of myself in a lowered position, humbled and honoring him with this physical show of expression and my great love for him.

I had a dream/experience that I want to share, and I pray that my words will not be misconstrued. It is hard to share something so personal and it has the deepest of feelings attached to it, please know that I consider this lesson as a sacred teaching and repeat it here in that context.

In my dream/experience, I was going to have the opportunity to meet and speak with Jesus. At the very sight of him, I began to kneel just as I always thought I would, but Jesus would have none of it, and he quickly extended his hand to bring me off of my knees. As he did this, he looked directly at me as he spoke the following words:

> *"Do not kneel before me, as i do not ask you or any other to worship and kneel before me. What i ask is that you stand beside me, and walk with me as friend and fellow teacher."*

It has taken me awhile to speak of this experience, choosing to keep it close to my heart as I reflected on the power and simplicity of his words.

I still look at my beautiful picture of Jesus every day, but now I look at it in an even more familiar way than I ever did before. I see him as more of a friend now, and not as a deity to be worshiped. I do my best every day to continue his teachings, working steadfastly towards the day I am able to walk beside him.

Inadequate

in·ad·e·quate

/inˈadikwət/

Adjective

Lacking the quality or quantity required; insufficient for a purpose.

"These labels prove to be wholly inadequate."

Synonyms: insufficient, not enough, deficient, poor, scant, scanty, scarce, sparse, too little, too few, short, in short supply.

(of a person) unable to deal with a situation or with life.

In the early years of my spiritual quest, I was completely sincere in my willingness to learn and to serve. I studied endlessly and prayed for my own personal connection to God. I wanted to be like the people in the spiritual books I was reading, because they seemed to be so much further along on the path then I was.

I spent my evenings watching YouTube talks and going to seminars of fellow NDE'rs who had a full story to tell their audience. I made it a point to meet and become friends with many of them, and I asked serious questions of them, because I was trying to understand what made them so different from me. Why did my NDE experience seem so lacking of a good plot and strong writeable ending?

To me, it appeared that they were so much closer to God, and well on their way through their spiritual journey, and I questioned why I seemed to be lagging so far behind? Wouldn't God want to answer my questions by putting me on the fast track of advancing seekers? Hadn't I proved a sincere desire?

Then I had the following dream lesson.

I was to climb a mountain with a group of other climbers. I was new at this, but very excited to do it. I was so happy as I prepared for the climb, until I noticed what everyone else was wearing, and I looked to my own clothing which now seemed totally inappropriate.

I did not match the kind of serious 'gear wear' the others wore, though I thought I had looked quite fashionable at home as I dressed. But now the scarf around my neck seemed more suited for a luncheon than mountain climbing.

The more I compared myself to everyone around me, the more uncomfortable I became, and although this was more of a day trip than a big Everest type climb, I realized that I was going to feel uncomfortable about myself all day.

I started fidgeting with my gear, keeping my head down as my confidence level dropped. I still wanted to go, but I was also busy creating my own kind of misery as we grouped together for the last bit of instruction before our ascent.

Our attention to the instructor was interrupted by a woman who was brought into the group on a stretcher. She had come to climb by way of ropes and pulleys.

I noticed that she was dressed perfectly in the mountain climbing gear that would rival any catalog cover, but she would be making the climb laying on her back. I watched in amazement as she showed no signs of feeling less than or inferior in any way, and I had to ask myself, if she doesn't feel inadequate, why do I?

Why do I have a tendency to get into my own head and sabotage my own progress, and why do I hold my own self back? And I remembered other ridiculous comparisons I had made in my lifetime.

How could this woman on a stretcher look beyond the capabilities of her body and imagine herself getting to the top of a mountain?

I knew right then and there while still within the dream, that I was to stop considering myself limited or inadequate. I woke knowing I had been taught a valuable lesson, and never again would I compare myself or the pace of my progress against anyone else's.

Ego and Self-Esteem Spirit School

"SHOW YOURSELF" were the words I heard during this vivid teaching dream.

It began with what looked to be boxes stacked together in rows of at least five across and five deep. Upon closer examination, I saw they were really individual screens, and each one contained a different person, or shall I say, a representation of that person.

As I watched, I noticed that each screen showed something different, though each was a living reflection of the individual who inhabited the space. In all honesty, it looked a lot like the intro to the Brady Bunch.

Some of the people were difficult to see because they were standing behind a display of flowers, having decorated their screen with them. Other boxes showed a person standing full on and facing the screen while holding something in their hand. Other screens were almost completely blacked out, like they had taken a marking pen to color the glass of the screen.

It took me awhile to understand the meaning of the boxes, but as I interacted with them, I was made to see, that what a person puts out front, is not necessarily who they really are inside.

For example, the flowery ones had created a perfect persona as their disguise. They will smile and shake your hand and profess from the roof tops that they are doing great, but inside they are not. They hide a fragile esteem because they have been hurt, and they protect themselves by putting on a brave and overly friendly face for the world to see. It will take a lot of work before they will trust enough to ever show themselves as less than beautiful and perfect.

The ones with the blacked-out screens had created a hardened shell, and this protection of themselves kept them from connecting with others almost completely. Those that were the hardest to see were the ones who needed love and connection the most, but their shell kept them safe from all contact. For these types there is rarely an entrance, even though they need it more than they may know it themselves.

The ones that stood unabashed and facing the screen were showing a true identity, there was no need to decorate themselves. Their screen was bright and clear and led the way to their open heart. The small bag or neck piece they wore contained their ego, and one of the most important parts of the lesson was shown by the following words:

"CARRY YOUR OWN EGO IN A SMALL SATCHEL."

Since this class on Ego and Self-esteem in Spirit School, I have learned to be more mindful of who a person really is. Are they hiding behind the facade they present? I will work even harder to give understanding to the ones who openly hide behind it.

Hello, Soldier

One night I woke in a darkened room from a dream I could not remember. Going back to sleep was proving to be difficult and after a while I began to talk to my guide, playfully whispering, "It's been kind of quiet around here lately, can you send me a few words of encouragement?" And almost immediately I heard these words reverberate in my head:

"HELLO SOLDIER."

It reminded me of a time a few years ago under similar circumstances when I asked what was needed of me, and that I wanted to serve God in any way that I could, and I heard:

"BOOTS ON THE GROUND, WHERE CELESTIAL PAVEMENT ENDS."

I am not exactly sure what I am doing to be called a soldier, but I liked hearing it, and feel like I must be contributing a service in my own way. I fell asleep wondering about my role as a soldier, a way-bringer or carrier of light, and one who sees, as all of these terms have been used in my direction as an explanation of my earthly role. These terms all seemed so vague for my need of literal translations, and so I let them roll around in my head until I slept and dreamed of the answer to my question. I was to be a bridge.

Becoming a Bridge,
Its Importance and Responsibility

The veil has been thick for so very long, and this was an intentional design as we came to Earth to play the game of separatism and separation. We are here, away from all we know and understand, just as the souls on the Other Side who have not incarnated here have been left to guess what it is like to experience Earth.

The veil is thinning deliberately for both sides now; those curious souls are coming to see us more clearly with the help of a bridge of consciousness between the two sides.

A literal bridge across the divide, and a type of representative for both sides. This is to become my role.

Earth life is an opportunity to explore more of who and what we already are, but in a different experience of reality. It is made different by passing through the veil of forgetting when we birth into the human experience and enter the Earth game.

I was shown how important this role is to be 'THE BRIDGE', the in-between of the perceived separation caused by the veil, and its limiting communication with Spirit. The Earth game is more of the forgetting game, that we are all one, and instead, you believe that you are here alone, with limited resources, and countless questions.

"Why would I do this?" you may find yourself asking. The answer is in seeing the Earth game clearly, which is to see that:

    d. It is a prize only taken on with a great level of awareness.
    e. It is a game only played by great masters seeking new levels of experience.
    f. You came here not only willingly but with great excitement.
    g. As you consciously dissolve the veil of forgetfulness, you can teach others.

The depth of the experience can be shared and taught through us, the third party, the in-between, THE BRIDGES.

I was told, "You are the bridge between the other two consciousnesses, those who are still playing the game in the complete state of forgetfulness, and those on the Other Side trying to experience this game."

It was a lot to take in, but this teaching gave me a better understanding of the service I am trying to provide. I just didn't know how to describe it, even within myself.

It also gave some clarity to the other names I have been called over the last few years of my awakening, including being called a soldier by my trusted friend and spiritual guide, Click Click.

A bridge, a foot soldier, a way shower, a seer and a light bringer, haha, I guess since he allows me to call him Click Click, he can call me anything he wants.

The Act of Balance

In these times of our great dismay and the seemingly endless array of hate speech and violent acts, may I offer that there is an abundance of positive energy being poured onto Earth at this time. Rarely are acts of love and kindness reported in the daily news, as they are somehow of less interest than the rising death toll involving guns or the premeditated actions of thoughtless divisionaires and war mongers.

Unspeakable acts of darkness and negativity are quietly being counter balanced with actions that are unseen. Nevertheless, a balance of energy IS being maintained.

As the world receives this abundance of love and positive vibration, an exchange needs to take place requiring a delicate dance of the balance of energy. Darkness IS being released, and now more than ever it is essential that it be cleansed and purified and redirected back to Earth.

My dream experience showed a large green field, and in several areas a type of valve came out of the ground. I found myself standing next to a structure drilled deep into the Earth.

This pipe was so pristine that it lent itself an almost God-like quality in its mechanical efficiency and cleanliness. It was purposeful and it was important.

I was so drawn to it, reaching my hand out to touch it, and I discovered it was not a man-made interworking machine of steel covered in lubricating grease, but instead found it to be void of even a mark of grime.

There was something coming out of the top of this pipe, a foggy vapor in an orange/pink opaque color, but it was not fire or magma, and it was not hot to the touch. I was made to know that this was a representation of release for maintenance of harmonious balance. There are many of these valves placed with much forethought and purpose in key locations around the world.

I woke knowing that what I had witnessed was an important teaching example, and a metaphor for my understanding, But what came next, was a wonderful wakeful visual of the actual God-like valves working for the Earth's balance of energy.

The Valves Are Us

There are so many living and working receptacles placed in strategic areas around the Earth. Beams of light and love that counterbalance the negative acts.

Many of us are experiencing terrifying or at least curious dreams that upon waking, can be disturbing as you found yourself the star in an uncharacteristic role of crime, murder and betrayal. Do not despair, your dream was important and it gave exit to dark energy, released through you, in your sleep, and returned to God for restructure and cleansing into positivity.

It is important work, and one of the jobs of being a light worker or foot soldier of God is to carry the mantle of balance. It is very hard work, especially if you do not understand where these dreams originate, giving pause and some concern to your own sanity.

Usually these dreams will fall in number as you weary of having them, as they a carry considerable weight. But I feel confident saying that no one is given more than they can handle.

I found this comforting information after taking the place of the victim in several unspeakable dreams. I knew that they were not a past life recall, and that my role was short-lived so to speak, but I would wake up upset and exhausted, and unable to explain why.

I will give an example of one of the dreams that I was able to verify.

It was of two young brothers and a friend going camping together. Their hidden intent was to hunt bear, and they found themselves deep in an unfamiliar area where they could both feel and smell the presence of many of them. They were in big trouble and they knew it.

I played the part of the younger brother whose love and blind allegiance had me follow the older of us into this area of so much danger. When he told me to stop and be quiet, I understood the fear in his voice, and I knew to listen. On the other hand, the third boy was a friend, and his personality different from mine. He was loud and full of blame, "Now you've done it! Where are we? Oh, this is just great! This was your idea! Thanks a lot! Were all gonna die now!" He was in full on Bill Paxton form. His fear would not let him or anyone else think. He was unable to follow instructions, and he could not stop talking long enough to listen. There was only one old shotgun between them, and moments later, they were gruesomely attacked, mauled and ripped apart by a considerable number of their prey. Needless to say, this was a completely devastating dream and I ran to the bathroom to compose myself.

As I sat on the pot, a clear vision came into view of a tent set up in a front yard and three young men horsing around with each other and enjoying the planning of their upcoming trip.

I saw it by way of an old 8 mm film playing in front of me on the bathroom wall. I had a familiarity with this type of film as I grew up in the 60's, but because I was seeing it in color, I thought it to be of the early 1970's.

A father stood nearby with a hose in his hand. He had no idea of the extent of the boys' plans and what they were really up to or he would never have permitted them to go. I saw the love between these brothers and their friend in happier times and then the scene faded.

I was enthralled with all that I had witnessed, and I began to Google 'brothers killed by bears', and 'Three boys killed by bears in the 70's' and I found an article about two brothers and a friend in Canada who had been killed together in a seemingly senseless bear attack. The scene was gruesome and it tore the town and families apart. Blame was rampant as they searched for the missing boys, the anguish of them not returning home, and then discovering their resulting deaths and gruesome remains.

I could not believe what I was reading, or the fact that I was forced to play a part in this. What was the cruel purpose of my needing to witness and to feel the primal fear of these boys as they faced the horror of what was to become of them? I had no personal attachment to them, had never heard of this incident before, and I am not a hunter. I could go on and on of my whys, but WHAT WAS THE PURPOSE OF MY WITNESSING THIS HORIBLE ACT?

Frankly I was a bit pissed off by it all. Yes, I was happy to exercise a gift of 'seeing' and experiencing wonderful teachings from my guide in a heavenly classroom. I had gratitude for so much being given to me, but this, I did not understand this, and I reluctantly recorded it in my dream journal.

Not until this latest teaching of release was I able to put this puzzle together.

I was made to understand that this place on the Earth had been filled with much negativity, and although the bears were in a natural setting, the gruesome deaths, the physical fear involved, and the following breakdown of a close-knit community and warring of families, had created so much darkness, that this forest setting needed to be cleansed and purified.

The boys were long gone and their souls were at peace, this need was not of their making, but only of the energy of the tragedy that remained there in a constant flux of darkness, and it was time for it to be purified and released.

I had somehow accepted this assignment, as I am sure many of you have accepted similar agreements. You help by being a beacon of light, and your dreams work to release and reset energy, removing what had been negative in the form of a sanctioned release, and allowing light and positivity back in its place.

Hello Soldier.

7

Do Not Let Fear Become Your Story

It does not serve you

Letting Go of Fear

As a young child I was terrified to be alone in my room. My mother would spend many nights dutifully sitting at the end of my bed reading the newspaper until I fell asleep. I could never fully explain what I was afraid of. I was seeing things that were not easy to describe. My gift of seeing and hearing the dead did not seem like such a gift to this little girl.

My go-to answer was ghosts. I often saw them in my room, or at least in my field of vision. Though one night two figures stood at the end of my bed, a male and female. They were almost unisex looking, as there wasn't much difference in them. Their faces were white, and they wore long black tunics, which was a sharp contrast to the long white hair they wore to the shoulders. This visitation was more pronounced than what I was growing accustomed to seeing; it was more physical in nature. I didn't feel like they were trying to harm me, but I was terrified just the same. I couldn't make myself scream, though a low groaning noise came from somewhere within me. My mother must have heard it because she came in, and they abruptly disappeared into the wall. The main hallway was on the other side of this wall, and a metal doorbell box was attached snugly to it. For years I imagined they were hiding in it, just waiting for me to be alone in my room again.

I offer this description of one of my childhood fears in hopes of helping you face some of yours, of what goes bump in the night at your home, or in your mind.

After years of religious conditioning, I began to fear the devil too. In 1974 I watched the movie 'The Exorcist' at a drive-in theatre. My then husband insisted on sitting through this horrible movie twice. I was expecting my first child, and my hormones were already out of whack, and I began to have dark dreams of entrapment. These dreams carried on for years and years, and I would ask God or Jesus to help save me from the evil one.

I would practice trying not to think of anything 'bad' especially when sleeping alone. I would try not to give 'him' any thought at all, as this would tempt fate and then he would surely show up.

There were dreams when he did show up, and the room would spin and twirl. The lights would flicker off and on as the curtains billowed and the bed would shake. When I finally woke up, I would lay shivering in sheets soaked with cold sweat, with gratitude that I was OK.

As I became more spiritually connected, I started to let go of a belief that the darkness was as strong as the light. I no longer believed in hell for that matter, as I came into knowing that this belief was a form of control to corral us into following an earthly leader. I grew tired of the tall tales, and hearing that you had only this one chance to prove you can be a godly person in this hard world of duality. You must rise against all forms of temptation; you must be good or you will go to Hell,

In the church I had grown up in, even the diet coke I secretly enjoyed was going to send me there in short order.

I spent years in a quest for answers because I just could not believe that my short list of infractions were really worthy of my forever damnation to hell. The God I know in my heart is loving, and I call him my Heavenly Father, as this is the highest title of respect I know. I just could not envision him as an ego-driven deity who would throw his beloved children to the gallows for mistakes.

I began to focus on God as a friend, and I began to leave out the *thees* and *thous* in my prayers, as these words were not a part of my modern language. When I used them I felt false, and that only aided in keeping a distance between us.

Instead, I found that when I treated him as a friend, I could talk to him anywhere or anytime. The ritual of nightly kneeling was not necessary to show my love and respect, because I loved and respected him everywhere. I began to have real conversations with him, and I even began to talk to him in short sentences, like an ironic, "Oh geez, thanks for another red light" when I was already running late, or I would give a short "thank you" for the open parking spot near the front door in the rain. I found the formal prayer stuff was not needed to feel him near me, as I really did and still do feel him near me always.

As I grew more confident, the dark dreams began to subside. They came with less frequency, and in each one, I began to face the opponent with a strength that was my own, because I knew without a doubt that God was near me. I could tell the darkness that it had no power over me anymore. I knew in absolute certainty that God loved me, and that gave me more strength than Satan ever had over me.

My last devilish nightmare was in 2013. Some six years have passed since I stood in the middle of the room that was being upturned by evil. It was the same windy room with things being tossed about and hanging pictures twirling on their own accord, and I asked myself, "What's the worst thing that can happen here? Death?" and I followed this with a snippy and ironic "I've already done that." I had experienced the afterlife in my near-death experience, and it was pure bliss, and so I decided to let the power of the light take over, and I bravely said aloud, **"SHOW YOURSELF!"**

A figure in flowing black garb began to blow towards me. It was huge in stature, and I looked up, trying to see a face, but it was covered in darkness. I took a deep breath, and with my newfound strength of the power of the light to back me up, I stood tall as I shouted towards it, **"GOD LOVES ME!"** the words coming from the deepest depths within me. I will admit that the words came outstretched... seemingly in slow motion, and in lower volume than I had hoped, but the tone was serious, and I added, **"LEAVE ME ALONE, YOU DO NOT SCARE ME ANYMORE!"** And with that the Devil/Satan began to shrink before my very eyes.

The cape of dark cloth blew away, and his stature began to cave in. He was no longer taller than me, nor was he as wide and strong. His head was revealed, and I was surprised to see that he was balding. There was little hair clinging to the sides of his small head, and just a few long sprigs stuck out of the top of his shiny bald dome. Oversized horned rimmed glasses now covered his face, and they were held up by his pointy nose. His hands and shoulders began to curl into the fragile rickety bones of an old man that required a cane to walk.

With my fear no longer feeding him, he lost his power over me, and he became more of a cartoon figure. His ancient true self showed me that he is just a tired old man who knows what scares us.

I do not disparage the effects of fear. It can be made real, but it doesn't have to rule over you. You have a choice to give it power, or not. Cases can be made of the many things in this world that can hurt you, but to live in a state of fear is not healthy. Anxiety-driven bouts of fear and depression can become a story you tell yourself and those around you. I have seen Facebook groups that are based on fear, many giving all of their power over to it, and allowing it to govern their very lives.

Do not let fear become your story.

Right Turns Only

The mother of one of my dear childhood friends was participating in our school's carpooling effort, but after riding with her a couple of times, I began to notice something odd about her driving. She would not make a left-hand turn. For whatever her reasoning, she would drive some five miles out of her way, making only right-hand turns to get to the destination.

After exiting her car late for school one morning, I asked my friend about it, and she told me she didn't know why, but her mother was deathly afraid of stopping in traffic and turning left.

It seemed an odd thing to be afraid of to me, and I didn't understand the depth of her fear until one afternoon something happened that would force her to make this dreaded maneuver. She began to freak out, yelling and crying at the same time. She was kind of losing it, right there in front of all of us. I had never witnessed a parent so distressed before. The reasoning didn't matter, it was all very real to her, and she was terrified at being forced to face a fear that had festered inside of her for some time.

I could do nothing but watch my young friend talk her through it, using love and support in her voice to calm her down, even as the cars lined up behind us and angrily honked their horns in our direction. Hers was a voice of reason, and her mother began to respond, as she got her to take a deep breath and look ahead for the opportunity to turn. They walked through her fear together, and her mother made the turn and was then able to safely pull to the side of the road.

I can remember trying to act as if nothing had happened while she composed herself. I looked away, down at my shoes, and then out the window. I didn't want to add to the embarrassment she was expressing now.

This incident may seem a small thing or perhaps insignificant to others, but to her, this was a life changing event, as one of her biggest fears was being conquered through her daughter's calming voice. I watched the color come back into her face as she let this fear go, and I realized that left unchecked, fear could take on a life of its own and express itself with a darkness that can take over one's own will.

The fear that had ruled her for so many years had probably started in a seemingly small incident, but with each objection to face it, it began to feed itself. Each right-hand turn that took her further away from her destination acted as a stimulator to its growth, and into the disproportionate anxiety that now controlled her life.

I am not toting myself as an expert on how to dislodge fear, but I am asked to write about it, and to identify it, as we should not let fear be our ruler, and we should never surrender our own free will to it.

Solo

I have written of my son Jesse before, because I admire his true warrior spirit, though as a child he was also plagued by nightmares of the dark side. These dreams angered him more than they frightened him, and he would go into full battle mode in these dreams, fighting to keep himself and his family safe from harm, a big job for a young boy.

Jesse developed an inner strength through these dark dreams, and he has learned to use adrenaline, the by-product of fear, to serve him on the mountainside as he became an avid climber.

We sat together one evening, watching an amazing documentary on the history channel, called 'Solo' the story of Alex Honnold and his fearless free climb of El Capitan, the famous face of Yosemite.

Free climbing means no ropes or hooks or safety nets below. We watched spine tingling scenes of his dangling some 7,500 feet above the trees, hanging on without anything but pure grit and his fingernails.

Jesse used this opportunity to share his photo albums of many of his own documented climbs, and he talked of having met or climbed with many of those assisting Alex, and other honored climbers that were mentioned in the film.

Jesse had never spoken to me of his 'free climbs.' I guess he was sparing me a mother's worry, but I was facing it with him now, and I asked him about fear in general, and I was struck by his answer.

He told me there is no room for fear as you climb because your mind is always filled with the next three steps ahead. Not just the next step, because once there, you may not have another move, and you could find yourself stuck and in a life-threatening situation, so you must plan ahead, focusing on the next three moves, and there is no room to think of anything else.

The height is not an issue, as you already know how high up you are, and that is precisely why you are there. There is no fear as you look down, as that is a part of the climb, even in an almost upside-down move while sliding your fingers into a slender crack in the face of the rock.

You would think that the visuals alone would render them frozen with fear, but a free climber has practiced, and visualized this climb a thousand times. They have conditioned their body, and they are mentally prepared for what they are doing. He told me that fear has no place within that conditioning, and a climber who fails is prepared for that too, as death is an accepted consequence of a mistake of placement or a simple accident of nature giving way.

A climber does not carry any of these thoughts with them; thoughts of fear and failure are left at home. What is left is the thrill of the accomplishment of everything you have worked for coming together as planned and practiced, and then executed and achieved. One mountain down, another hundred to go.

As our discussion was coming to a close, he reiterated that he does everything he can do before the climb to ensure a good outcome, and it was now up to him to fulfill his quest and achieve success. But if something were to go terribly wrong, fear would only hinder his ability to think clearly to find a solution, and so fear never enters the mind of a climber. He left me with one of his Vikingisms: *"If this is the day you are to die, then it is a good day to die, and if it is your time to die, you did it while doing something you loved to do."*

I appreciated his lesson about fear, but as his mother, I asked him if it was OK that I still worry a little.

Squishing Arachnophobia

Last week I spent the afternoon playing in the backyard with three of my grandchildren. Jude was on the trampoline as Addison and baby Sawyer toddled and played in the yard.

Plopping down on the grass to take a break from chasing them, I reached out for Addie as she ran toward me. I beckoned her to sit next to me for some cuddles, but she told me that she would not sit on the grass. "Why?" I asked, and she answered that she was afraid to. "Honey, why are you afraid of the grass?" And she retorted, "because there are spiders in there."

I was a little dumbfounded that she was already expressing fear at such a young age, and I pulled her onto my lap and gave her a good grandma squeeze, and then I asked her, "What if a spider was crawling on my leg right now?" She began to squirm away at the very thought of that. As I held on, I reassured her by showing that there really was not a spider, and I asked her to play a game with me called 'Suppose there was' and what should we do then?

She was quiet as she gave it some thought, and when several moments passed without a reply, I said, "If a spider was on my leg right now, I would do this," and I calmly swept my hand across my leg as if to gently whisk the spider away. "See honey, I didn't even feel it, with just a soft flick, it would be gone, and it didn't hurt me and it didn't hurt the spider either." She stayed in my arms as I asked, "Would that be a good idea?" Then I had her practice this maneuver, first on my leg and then on her own.

Time will tell if this brief encounter will help Addie with her fear of spiders, but I did notice later after she had ridden her bike in a multitude of circles, that she sat down... on the grass... Humm, maybe a break-through here. I had hope.

> *A reminder*
> *not to believe in weakness or in fear*
> *but to restore a belief in yourself*
> *by accepting that you are*
> *a teacher of light in the making*

I woke to these words while writing this chapter, and within an hour a friend and fellow author sent the following quote. Happenstance, serendipity, synchronicity, coincidence, it has been called many things, but God is aware, and if we pay attention, we will recognize his gentle nudges in all we do.

> *Many people are afraid to heal because*
> *their entire identity is centered*
> *around the trauma they've experienced.*
> *They have no idea who they are outside of trauma,*
> *and that unknown can be terrifying*

How Do I Get out of Here, Where Do I Belong, and What the Heck am I Supposed to be Doing?

In January 2017, I had one of those 'I'm not prepared and I'm anxious' dreams that seem to go on and on. You know the kind. You are among your peers and dressed entirely inappropriately for the occasion, or perhaps not even dressed at all. You can't find your way, or you just can't seem to finish getting ready and out the door; you are already late while everything is going wrong.

I used to categorize these types of dreams as just stress, or nonsensical release dreams, but I have changed my mind. There is purpose in bringing one's self to a state of nervous energy and angst, and much can be learned from the experience.

In my dream, I found myself wandering in the hallway of a high school. I felt like I was sixteen again as I opened the door to a classroom full of students. They were all seated on tall stools in front of a white television box (yes, a computer but it was being used differently). Their faces were looking directly into it and for some reason it felt like the computer was attached to the mind of the specific person using it.

No one looked up as I came in, as they were busy taking some kind of test. I had no idea what the test was about, or at which table I should sit to find MY computer, or how to attach myself to it, or how to even turn the darn thing on.

I knew I should ask someone, but when I was in school I had a fear of looking stupid, and for some reason, I would rather get a poor grade than draw attention to the fact that I didn't understand something. Fear is a funny thing, and how and when this got started, I am not sure, but it was left unchecked and continued to grow disproportionately out of control. I even began to hold myself back from trying new things just in case I didn't perform perfectly on the first try.

I thought about sitting down and just pushing buttons until I got it to work, but fear is not rational. I knew this would surely draw attention to myself and my dread of not knowing all the answers. I considered going to the counselor's office, but worried that I might be punished for not being prepared. I wondered how far behind everyone I would be by the time I got it figured out, and so I slipped out the door in my usual fashion, thinking it was easier to forget about it than to jump in late and fail. Failing on my own terms was my chosen option.

I went to a library area, and it was full of white- and silver-haired people seated at regular sized tables and chairs. They were all working on something without a computer, but I felt I didn't belong in this room either.

As I walked down the hallway, I found myself looking through a window to an outside stadium or arena, where masses of people were cheering. They were watching some kind of game that I didn't recognize. It wasn't football or any other game one would normally see on a school field, and again I was confused and felt left out. Should I stay or should I go?

Where did I belong in all of this? The visuals of this dream were so real, and the feelings it evoked were fear and frustration. Had there been a schedule, and had I missed it? What was I supposed to be doing, and where was I supposed to be doing it?

I continued down the hall and found the classroom of a trusted teacher. I have thought of Mrs. Mitchell many times over the years, an English teacher who loved my essays and often told me so. She made me feel good about my writing, though she would always ask why I hadn't written about the death of my father that had occurred earlier in the year. I wished I could tell her that it was not yet time for me to speak of it. I had not come to grips with it yet, it was just too big and emotionally charged. And so I would just shrug my shoulders and say, "I dunn know" and would hope she liked what I had written instead.

So now in my dream, I am in front of her desk, and although I liked and trusted her more than any other teacher I knew, I was not sure about asking her where I belonged or what I was supposed to be doing, and if I had missed something.

So many frantic thoughts ran simultaneously through my head, but she seemed to understand my confusion as if she had heard me speak, and she asked, "What about your book?" There was a long pause of surprise before I answered "What? My Spiritual book?"

How did she know I was thinking of writing a book? She heard my thoughts and answered, "Yes, the book you are to write." And then I woke up.

I had not spoken about my thoughts of writing a book to anyone else but my trusted friend Charlene. She alone had been instrumental in the idea of gathering my stories together in a binder. I wasn't sure how it would all come together, or if my own family would even be interested in reading it, thinking that maybe my stories were just for me or a few close friends. I wavered back and forth in my thinking; was I ready to put myself 'out there?'

After waking I lay there thinking about this confusing dream, and I slipped into another.

This time my guide was present and wearing another of his 'pay attention and remember' costumes.

He looked quite dapper in a Jack Kerouac (author of 'On the Road') kind of way, wearing a black turtleneck sweater and slacks. He was holding something out towards me, and he pushed it towards my hands several times before I finally took hold of it. It was a typewriter, and although he spoke no words, I knew in that moment I had found what I was supposed to be doing.

I knew my purpose. I was to write a book, and it would be filled with what I had learned, and what I knew to be true. I was to stand fearlessly as I presented it to the masses, and I completed that book by the end of that year. 'GIFTS FROM THE EDGE Stories of the Other Side,' was published by November 2017. I am as proud of it as anything I have ever accomplished, stepping outside of my fears, and out of my own way.

I have learned not to run away from what scares me, and I stand firm as I ask the deepest of questions. WHY AM I HERE? WHO IS GOD? WHERE DO WE GO AFTER THIS LIFE IS OVER? WILL I STILL BE ME? CAN MY LOVED ONES ON THE OTHER SIDE HEAR ME WHEN I CALL OUT TO THEM? AND WILL YOU HELP ME TO 'HEAR' THEM IF THEY CALL OUT TO ME?

I offer the answers to these questions and more in the books that I write, with a full understanding that they are my purpose, and that I am guided to do it. But most importantly, I have learned to face my fears, and I am no longer afraid to ask for help when I need it.

8

Reincarnation, The Big Picture

" No matter how hard it may seem
Each forward step will give you
Strength to take another.
A journey begins
By placing one foot in front of the other."

- Claudia Watts Edge

Are you ready to step into oneness?

As I worked on this chapter of living many lives, this wonderful, concise and straight-to-the-point explanation of reincarnation popped onto my screen. It was a post from Rod H. McCallum Jr. a seeker and a friend, answering many of the questions of the why, 'Why would we put ourselves through this experience over and over again?' I am always amazed at the perfect timing of spirit, and with Rod's permission, I offer it here as synchronicity at its finest.

This Life IS the Next One You Wanted To Do

Please excuse my language - all of the shit, the heartache, the pain, the envy, the confusion, the anxiety, the doubt, the fear... mark my words - you will miss all of it.

Yes, of course you'll miss sunsets or sunrises, babies, flowers, the sun... that's obvious. And you THINK you're going to be so happy to be rid of the difficult parts of your journey here - but you are WRONG. You will absolutely miss all of the crap. All of that spice and flavor that is part of life.

Because you see the polarity - one has the good and bad, the sweet and sour, but all of it is the journey. And you miss all of it. You long to be in form again and again.

See, once you leave here - there is no pain, there is no suffering, there is no doubt, no confusion.

You stop and go "Oh wow. Look how much I got caught up in all that drama. Look at how I would get worried and feel unsure. Ha Ha Ha. I didn't know what was going on then. If only I knew... oh, yeah, I guess it wouldn't have been the same experience if I knew what was going on.

Ah, now I see. Now I understand. It's all so beautiful. It's so perfect. That was amazing. I thought it was so real.

Well, that life was an interesting experience. I wonder what I want to do next. What's the next adventure I can try." And so, for you the perspective is clear. It's the highest perspective of knowing all that's happening is what you wanted to experience. And so, the question always ends up being the same - what do you want to do next? This life you have right now is that "next one" you wanted to do.

- Rod H McCallum Jr.

A Visual of Our Many Lives

During a teaching dream, I found myself standing at the base of a very large downed tree.

The trunk had been sawed into two halves; the clean cut revealed the middle of the tree, and the perfectly smooth rings that grew to create the tree's grain.

There were hundreds of these circled lines held within the thick protective bark of the tree; I ran my hand over them, each one so very different from the ring before.

Some were thicker, others were darker, and some were faint and wispy looking. I was so drawn to them, each one of them unique in their own right. Running my hand over them, I began to trace them, and I was made to know that this was a visual representation of 'MY OWN LIVES.' All the lives that I had lived before were connected to and a part of the tree, the tree that was the representation of Me.

Hidden inside the rough outer layer were the many individual yet connected rings of my lives. They were all playing their part in making up the whole of me and who I truly am.

Even the exterior, the last ring in the group that represented me now, was destined to become one of the many rings of the same tree.

It made so much sense to be able to see this, and I knew that I had been given a gift and a teaching tool. This picture helped me to understand and explain how necessary all of our lives are to the sum of our complete self, our higher self, and each ring is an important contribution to the whole of our being.

A 360-Degree View

In my meditations and prayers I ask for more, but not of this world. I ask to receive more pieces of the perpetual spiritual puzzle, and to understand what my part is within it. As I slide further into my sixties, I really want to know that I am accomplishing my mission, the reason and purpose I am here.

I am aware of and excited by the progression I have made. The years of research by book, by dream, by vision, by lesson, by service and life experience, by good times and dark times, loneliness and joy, and the wonderful gifts of like-minded friends placed along my path. I am so grateful for everything I have received, and yet I find myself asking for more. Like an addict, I need a fix, another connection, a heavenly hello or an atta boy, though I preface those asks, with an "I don't need it but I want it, and please sir, can I have some more?" And then there are the times I give a zealous, "I want to know more and see more!" I pray to achieve the most of the experience this time around, and I carry a feeling of being truly protected, nudged and guided.

There is much fun in the mystery of connecting the dots through dreams etc. It can become an addicting game, played with loving guides who are willing to share what they feel I am ready to know. They are ready to help me <u>IF I ASK</u>, and this is key, ASKING, because of our FREE WILL CONTRACT.

Nothing is forced upon us, and there is no 'right' path that we can fall from. Our path is an intended lesson/experience of our own choosing, and our journey was set up long before we arrived here. Who our parents are to be, and the country where we are to be born, are parts of well-orchestrated 'chances.' Who we meet, befriend or love, are all preset in a life course, with willing soul family participants taking on the starring roles.

All is worked out in advance, but none of it is set in stone. All is subject to our free will to make our own choices, and the choices are ours to make. Our charted course can be redirected, and this is the miraculous beauty of this earthly play we are participating in, and the roles we have chosen. Adjustments can and will be accommodated, and the experience of our intention can still have a successful outcome.

Nudges and Flashpoints

Some of the nudges we receive are preplanned flags of recognition such as a funny dance move, or the crooked smile of a new acquaintance. Something just feels familiar and a knowing happens, like Déjà vu. The feelings for this new dance partner quicken, as you almost immediately know that someday they will become your husband or wife.

A certain house on a seemingly familiar street where you feel you must live, could be one layer to build upon the pre-plan of your children's experience and on and on, and on.

It can keep you up nights trying to figure it all out because now that you are here, you can't remember for the life of you what the plan was. And that, dear reader, was another conscious decision made before your arrival.

We entered this life agreeing to be born through a veil of separation, creating a total amnesia of the grand nature of who we truly are, seeding human doubts and fears that we must work through. The unconditional love of our creator would not leave us here all alone without help, and so we come into the world with triggers or points of reference and recognition. They were planted within us for gentle pushes, set up long before our physical birth to affirm that we are indeed on course for our intended task. These implanted flashpoints help to ignite and steer us. But never are our lives on auto pilot with a set destiny or outcome. What would be the point?

We Are Not Set Up to Fail or Fall

We are not set up to fail and fall from God's grace, to be punished for not having lived a perfect spiritual life here. For that is what we came from—ABSOLUTE PERFECTION. We came here to experience IMPERFECTION, fear, pain, cold, fatigue, sex, indulgence, addictions, hunger, jealousy, rage, and illness, just some of the necessary dualities we face in this world.

The question looms: can we overcome hardships tossed our way with grace? Can we express love and show kindness and care for our fellow man in the midst of our own daily struggle for survival here? We had a hand in setting up our own stumbling blocks along the road, and what can be learned from them. Perhaps through our experience and personal knowledge, another headed down the same path can be helped.

Can we move forward with a greater understanding of what it took to overcome our fumbles, and move forward with an appreciation of our own accomplishments?

Will we share the fruits of the experience? Will planted stumbling blocks prove to be steppingstones along the road we travel?

The Big Life Exam

There is a big life exam, but it is not a test. There are no wrong answers, only the experience to be analyzed. The only judgment that takes place on the Other Side is during your 360-degree review, and it will be your own. Judgment is not the correct word either, because that is a man-made concept for accessing punishment, but for lack of a better word I will continue to use it here.

The punishment is being a witness to and re-living the life experience through the eyes of those who were affected by you. You may not have even or realized that you caused pain, but you will have the opportunity to feel those hurts and sorrows, and you will be mindful that it was your actions that created their distress. And that awareness will be judgment enough and punishment enough.

There is another perspective that will be experienced during the 360-degree view, of all the kindnesses shown and the helpful moments you created as well. You will also experience them through the eyes of those you affected, but this time the focus is on the good deeds you created. How wonderful to be able to see a difference you made in someone's life by a simple gesture of kindness. It may be one so seemingly small, that you may not even remember the incident. But a deep impact was made on a life and those around it, just like throwing a stone into a stream and watching the ripples push outward, each ripple affecting the next, expanding and growing larger as it gains momentum. There will be much joy in the review as you witness these ripple effects causing positive change, more than you ever realized while living in the flesh.

The Theatre of Life is a Gift

Be mindful that your life is a gift, and this THEATRE OF LIFE was created especially for you, by you and the spiritual advisors who love and know all of your strengths and weaknesses. The situations and players are poised to bring out the best and the worst in you, and they have many similarities to the holographic room of Star Trek fame.

The Earth is a masterfully crafted world of dualities, created with unconditional love, especially for us. It gives us opportunities to come back and play over and over again, each time with a chance to experience something entirely new. The players and roles can be reversed, the centuries changed, and even your gender switched for new perspectives and experiences.

Our greatest enemy here can be our closest confidant and friend on the Other Side, a part they played so well that you were brought to your knees in grief and pain while here. But after your earthly deaths, you will hold each other in embrace, with a slap on the back for a job well done. You really did 'hate' them as they drove you deeper into your own experience, and although hard to fathom now, you will one day say, "Bravo friend, well played!"

Earth-Life Theatre

I am including a picture here of the Earth-Life Theatre as it was shown to me in Spirit School. It is arched like a theatre, and the starring roles in the small half-circle are the handful of close family, friends, and lovers who will make their mark in your world for good and bad. They will play the intricate roles of longevity in your life arena and are generally from your closest family/soul group on the Other Side.

The rings continue outward, each a smaller role than the last, but all are important. Even the last rows, or the cheap seats of walk-on players with small one-line parts cannot be measured by a lesser degree of impact, because they represent the vehicle that will touch your life or help change its direction.

I am in awe of the love shown us by our Maker, the Creator/Source/God of this and the many untold worlds that were created for us to experience, grow and learn. That is our precious gift, and as we play, we learn, for there is no greater way to teach than by actual experience.

I am in gratitude for the love shown to us by the magnanimous undertaking in the creation of this beautiful physical world. We have been given the opportunity to experience all of it in a 360-degree continuation of lessons, that are carried back within us through the veil upon our physical death, to be shared with our Maker.

WE ARE HERE SO THAT GOD CAN EXPERIENCE HIS OWN IMAGINATION.

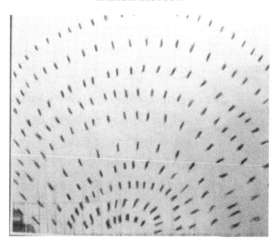

My Other Lives

I have mentioned viewing myself in various lives before, the vivid dream/experiences began to flow during and shortly after reading 'JOURNEY OF SOULS', by Dr. Michael Newton. I highly recommend looking into this book as a possible gateway into your own journey of understanding.

It was not my intent to include my own personal discoveries of 'my selves' when I began this book, perhaps still fearing judgment and ego, but I have been nudged to share some of the most vivid ones. And that heavenly push outweighs any of my earthly discomforts. My hopes in sharing them with you dear reader, is a step that will allow you to trust enough to explore the possibility of your own experiences beyond the one you are having now.

Why a need to know? you may ask, and you would be right in thinking that it is not a necessity to know, but for me it has been a valuable gateway into an understanding and aiding the purpose of THIS trip.

As I experienced each individual being/me, I recognized numerous lessons and experiences of betrayal, despondent sadness, wealth and loneliness, a fear-based life, a thoughtless and cavalier lover and a complete giving over of my own self-worth and freedom as I was shackled into slavery, just to name a few.

As I compile this list, one would wonder why we would want to come back for another round, or why would we put ourselves through all of it, and in earthly thinking I would agree. But in terms of eternal knowledge and experience, there is no better way to learn than to physically live it, taste it, and feel it, the pleasure and the pain equal in its experience.

We HAVE walked miles in another's shoes, and the 'another,' is us.

Studying reincarnation is a chance to know yourself while still here in the game, in this life, instead of the 360' degree overview on the other side after it is over. Call it an advantage in the understanding of what your goal may be in this life, and you can work within it and actively learn as you participate.

MIGELLA

My first recollection of another life came in a scene of a small boy around five or six years old. The recognition of him/me started with looking at my feet, as I remembered reading that this was a successful technique to visualize age and gender while having these kinds of vivid dreams/memories and so I focused my concentration there first.

My feet are small and bare and noticeably dirty. Continuing up, I see that my legs are covered with dried mud or worse. The visual advanced up my body until I found a sweet boy's face under a head full of curly brown hair.

I was near a rock wall, and beside it was a trench with spots of stagnant water, and green grass grew thick and tall around it. He/I was playing with a stick outside the city walls of... Rome? Cairo? I am not sure, but I knew I was not allowed beyond these walls or into the city behind them.

This scene took place over a thousand years ago, though it was bright and real in my recall, and I was completely lucid throughout. I reacted from within myself when I saw the soldiers riding up towards the gates near me. It was too late to run and I was afraid, telling myself over and over in a whispered voice to "stay small." I held myself ever so still in the act of trying to become invisible in the grassy ditches of the city sewers.

These soldiers were returning home riding huge horses, and still partially dressed in battle gear, though their heads were uncovered. One spotted me and called out as he looked at the stick I had been wielding as a sword in a pretend battle, and I realized with a shaking awareness, that I had drawn unwanted attention to myself. "COME HERE BOY!" The soldier's voice was big, and it seemed to carry thunder within it, but I did not dare to run. Instead, I slowly moved towards the men on horseback.

I took a full accounting of the one who spoke. He had greasy dark hair and a full beard. He wore a black shirt under his chest plate of pounded golden metal and his muscular arms were exposed. He was a magnificent looking giant of a man. As he looked down on me from his horse, he was smiling when he teasingly asked, "So you want to be a soldier do you?" I answered with a childlike confidence, "Yes!" He chuckled at my answer, turning to his compadres as he lowered his arm towards me and offered his hand. I knew it was his intent to pull me up to him, "Come, little soldier," and with that sound, I let go of my fear. I was going to ride into the city restricted from me, and I would be one of the respected warriors, and so I let myself be pulled up to sit behind him, feeling pride at my newly found position.

It was a wonderful feeling being so very high off the ground. My bare legs rubbed against the hot sweat of his beautiful black horse. I saw a hatchet braced against his back. I could smell a heavy mixture of smoke, wax, metal and grease, but I found it all a part of his strength and mystery, and so I basked in it. I was smiling ear to ear, and I was proud to be one of the city's newest soldiers.

We had only walked a few steps toward the marsh that was the sewer for the city, the dump, where my glory was to be short lived. Within a second in time and either a change of heart or a calculated cruelty, he turned and shoved me off like a gnat.

I flew off the horse's rump and landed with a twisted neck in the sewer below.

The last thing I heard on this Earth, was an echo of combined laughter as the soldiers continued through the gates. None of them even looked back towards the young boy, who was just one of the 'rubbish people,' as we were known.

There would be no accusations or judgment calls made of this act of taking my life.

It would be of no consequence to anyone but my mother, a woman with no husband, and no rights. We lived outside of the city walls as scavengers, in the poverty and the refuse of the garbage dumps and sewers. We were the dirty and poor who lived off of the cast-offs of others.

I would find myself rising above my little body in a state of confusion as my mother screamed my name over and over in mournful weeping. She would suffer my loss, her only child, and the cruelties inflicted by those who mattered, onto those who didn't.

INDIAN SLAVERY

I had an intense dream of the betrayal of a Native American Indian tribe. In this lifetime I was a woman, and this tribe was mine. We were gathered together in trust, and now we were being held against our will by Spanish speaking soldiers. Although we didn't understand their words, we knew we were to be brought back to their country as slaves.

I was living through a very personal anguish, as I relinquished my free self.

Our captors were using a rope system to 'hobble' us. Two sets of ropes were used, one on each side, tied in some kind of triangle about the waist to the foot. It enabled limited walking, needing one to move each side independently of the other, in kind of a swing step that would allow movement, but at a tiringly slow pace.

I was in the process of being hobbled when my captor became distracted and left me only 'half' hobbled. My left side was roped up, but not the right, and as I stood alone half-finished, I wondered if I could or should run? Was this my opportunity to escape? Or should I try to avoid the captor's glances, pretending to be fully finished, and make an escape later on, after formulating a real plan. What if I was spotted? Would it make it worse for me, my situation? Would I be killed or beaten and maimed for good?

The captor had not yet returned, and I stood alone with these agonizing life and death decisions as I waited to become a full prisoner.

This non-decision left me feeling like a wimp and a loser of self-esteem as I stood there like a mindless robot waiting for my captor to return and finish taking away my freedom.

I did not understand the cruelty that could be imposed on another human being, and my lack of response to it was against everything I knew of myself. I was losing everything; it was seeping and oozing out of me, my strength, my honor, my pride. It was the worst kind of punishment.

I woke without remembering anything more. Did I run? Or did I just stand there looking like a weak and willing participant? I guess in the end it didn't matter; my life was over either way, but the lesson of my indecision has weighed heavily on me.

HERNICK

During dreams of previous lives, I have become accustomed to looking down at my feet, at what kind of shoes I'm wearing, or if I am barefooted. And in this way, my gender can also be revealed.

This would not be the case in the following experience though, because as I became lucid, I clearly saw my hands because I was seated and my focus was on my fingers. They were short and pudgy, and each one held a ring of bulky gold and stones right up to the knuckle. I was male, but my elegant costume would rival the closet of any woman. I was wearing layers of detailed woven textiles in rich deep colors, and they were edged in fine gold trimmings.

I looked around and saw that I was sitting in a grand hall full of people in similar dress, and we were supping at huge tables full of rich food and drink. I realized that I was a part of the Kings Court, and this type of gathering was my daily way of life.

I was not a king, but only one of the numerous players in his court. And although my position had been long held, I knew I was not necessarily respected or valued. I seemed to be more of a fixture who held a meaningless title, and I was feeling so very tired and bored with all of it. My amusement seemed to be in the amount of food and drink I could consume at each evening's gathering.

Seated in a permanent spot next to me was my sister, who had my ear as she offered me waves of gossip or endless comparisons of who and what was fair or equal to what we had.

Her quest for power was unquenchable and it had physically tainted her beauty, and so neither of us were married, and I would suffer her relentlessly pushing and poking me towards a more elevated status. She was to be both my closest ally, and the bane of my existence.

Our lifestyle in the court was good, but it was all due to her backstage bargaining for my advancements. I would be forever trapped in her debt, and miserable for it. She would have nothing without the benefit of my gender, and her status would forever depend on me, the male heir to the family name. She would spend her life with the burden of being forever tied to a brother that really didn't want any of it, and yet was too lazy and too well cared for to leave its comforts. She felt the entrapment as well, and so the constant nagging and prodding was a necessary evil in her own mind.

The last misdeed I performed at her bidding was evicting a widowed woman and her two children from one of the properties I held. Her husband had been murdered, and she had no other family or means of support, and no-where else to go. I let my sister's greed usurp my own generous heart and I had the widow removed against her will, and my own. I felt a terrible guilt at what I had done. It was slowly consuming me, and I tried to fill the hollowed emptiness by filling my plate.

There was music and entertainment all around me, and the air was filled with joyful noise and laughter. But for me it sang of a falseness, a performance called happiness that I could not partake in. And so I would sit with plate after plate of food, and lick the grease from my thick fingers as I nodded to the droning sound of my sister's voice.

It was time to go, and I was drunk enough to find some solace in sleep. But before I could get to my room, my sister pulled me aside. I was forced to listen as she formulated a new plan, based on something she had just overheard while standing in the shadows. There was an excited energy in her voice as she described the domino effect of dishonor that would land us squarely in the king's good graces. Another betrayal was in the making, and I was to spearhead it. The thought of it sickened me, though I listened without offering any verbal protest.

I was finally able to break free by telling her we would refine the plan in the morning, and I found my way to the carved stone stairway that led to my chambers. I was finally away from the noise of the crowd and the sound of my sister's voice droning constantly in my ears until it reached deep into the confines of my brain.

I moved myself slowly up the steps, carrying the weight of the world and the excessive weight of myself. I took a wearied breath of acceptance of what I had become and of what I had never wanted to be, when the room began to swim, and I began to sweat profusely.

I found myself gasping for air that would not come into me, and I began to clutch at my chest. I was losing my footing on those finely chiseled steps, and I felt the girth of my own body in its entirety, crushing down on my lungs.

I woke from this vivid experience knowing I had reached the end of this lifetime when I had been born into a name of privilege and status, and yet in its reflection were my own misdeeds.

I was called Hernick, though I do not know if that was my first or last name, and I knew that I had destroyed my own heart and will, for the keeping of it.

TENNA

After listening to a relaxation CD by Dr. Brian Weiss, a past life regressionist and author of the acclaimed book *Many Lives Many*

Masters, I rolled over to go to sleep and saw a flash behind my eyelids and a living scene came into my view. I saw a beautiful quarry pond, deep within rocky canyon walls of lush greenery, and blue water.

The flash was the result of a man jumping into a pond from the rocky cliffs above, creating a large splash filled with water and sunlight. I witnessed this plunge from at least 100 feet away, while freely swimming to the other side of the quarry.

"I'm swimming in a quarry," I thought aloud. I had never done this in my life as Claudia, and only recognized this pond as being a quarry because I had seen one in the movies. But now as I lay in my bed, I can actually touch the cool water as it rolls over my body, and I can feel everything the swimmer/me, is thinking and feeling.

At the shore, I reach for my shoes, putting them on while I am wet, rather than risking getting my feet dirty. They are white/grey leather, shaped like a dancing slipper, with thin leather on both the top and bottom so I can feel the earth beneath my feet, and I love this feeling.

I run my fingers through my curly brown hair as I check my reflection in the water. I am female, and I notice my teeth first because there seems to be a lot of them, or my mouth is not large enough to hold them all. I am not a beauty, but I am handsome enough, and I carry a self-assured confidence that adds to my allure.

I am responsible for my own needs and wants, and I actively pursue both. A perfect example of my carefree attitude is how I can leave this gentleman behind by just swimming away, while he is busy climbing the cliffs to dive. I can leave him without so much as a thought or a goodbye, just because I feel like it.

I do what I want, I always have. And right now I want to run through the trees toward town and home. My own feet are the best way to travel, and I run almost everywhere, loving the feeling of softly pounding against the ground. I am happy and most satisfied to be me.

I am an unusually progressive woman of the time, somewhere in the 1800's, owner of a successful woman's apparel shop and an accountant for many other businesses. I have a head for numbers and for making money, though I have ruffled many feathers along the way for not behaving like other women in this time period. I am revered, and a point of contention among many.

A few yards down the trail I am met by a woman, and she is angry with me, saying she is tired of my cavalier attitude. I have treated her carelessly. She has been a lover, but now I am here with a man, and she is jealous and angry. I am cold and distant to her as I cannot find it within myself to identify with her pain. I cannot or will not give her the apology and exclusivity she is looking for. I am now bored of being yelled at, and my attention is drawn to the road ahead that will take me away. Ignoring her and turning my back to her, I take only a few steps before her rage takes over and she gives me a hard shove from behind. I lose my balance and my footing, falling forward over the canyon's edge to the rocks below. I am gravely injured and disoriented, and I cannot help myself for the first time in my life. I am broken and alone against the rocks, and I will suffer greatly for several days before my body is discovered.

An innocent man will pay for another's crime. It is an ugly and bitter end that will leave me laying helplessly, with time to think about my thoughtless mistakes as my impending death drags its heavy cloak over me.

I learned a valuable lesson in this life, to be mindful of what my true intentions are, and to be more thoughtful of other's feelings.

My name was Tenna and I was twenty-seven.

The Wheel of Lives

I have heard of the term *parallel lives*, and of the concept that time is not linear, but it was a struggle for my human brain to really comprehend. This illustration helped me to understand the concept. It came while I was doing a lot of driving, during my move from Colorado to Utah, weary from the road's hypnotic stream of white lines and passing scenery. When sleep finally came, it seemed to be a perfect time for my mind to just let go and be free to experience the most vivid of teachings.

I became lucid in a dream, and I watched as a huge circle slid into my visual plane. It was a wheel, and it was all dressed up in decorative iron work like you would see on a fancy front door. What I saw was an ornate, turning wheel, in intricate detail.

I was made to understand that this wheel represented my life right now; the elaborate scroll work represented the different facets of my life, and on close examination I noticed a smaller circle within the detail of the wheel. As the larger wheel continued to turn, I kept watching the smaller circle and saw that it too, was turning.

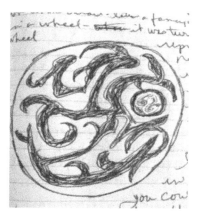

I was instructed to stay focused on the small circle, as this represented a window into the previous/parallel lives I was living, and so I fixed my gaze on the decorative circle within the decorative wheel.

Every now and then their turning coincided, leaving an opportunity for me to peek deep inside and see another of my lives as it was being lived.

It was amazing to realize that it was all somehow connected. It was difficult to witness this just by looking, but if I was patient and stayed focused, when the timing of both wheels turned to a brief eclipse and complete simpatico, there was an opportunity to 'see' in real time, something that until now I had called previous lives.

I now understand that the term 'previous' is incorrect, because without the constraints of a timeline, I am actually still living these lives, all at the same time.

I have heard that as we progress and advance, the things we learn and understand about ourselves will also have an effect on our other lives. They are not just a strict recording of history in a type of video. They are a continuing, adjustable learning tool, and we are equipped to reshape and actually redirect the outcome of those other lives with our positive advancements.

This was an amazing demonstration for me, and I wish I had artistic talents to share with you what I was shown, but I have included my own rendering, in the hope that it will facilitate your own understanding.

Choosing a Body

During a time of many focused teachings and personal discoveries in the field of reincarnation, I had the following dream-experience/memory. I was in Spirit School, and the lesson of the evening was 'The Progression of Choices' that we make before coming back.

As the lesson started, I saw myself with my son Jesse as we stood together in 'The Room of Choices.'

I was accompanying him as an equal and eternal soul friend, and also as one who would be greatly affected by the choices he was about to make.

We had reached the point of knowing that this time around, I would be coming in early to set the conditions to play the part of his mother. And he was now at the point to choose the likely adversities he would face, and the genetic probabilities of the body, the vehicle into which he would incarnate.

I would be instrumental in this decision, as his choice would determine many of my own life choices. Especially the options of location, and the partners with whom a union would allow for the possibilities of his body choice.

Layer upon layer is added in this process, building complicated details, textures and colors into the fabric of the lives being created. All is done with a desired end result in mind.

It is a painstaking job to weave this tapestry together, and no choice is taken lightly.

These decisions are made with much forethought and counsel, and with the consideration of those who will be playing a role in the life. Each choice affects all involved in a kind of domino effect. All needs must be considered in this wonderful opportunity of experience and education on Earth.

All participants for this cycle of life have their own choices, and everyone's needs have to be accommodated to achieve the most desirable and optimum outcome for all. And if all of this isn't enough, it all has to be accomplished knowing full well that our free will can and will take precedence over any pre-planning or coordinated efforts.

There are adjustments available for the use of free-willed changes, because there is always a possibility of partners not showing up, or an untimely accidental death, and even suicide has to be factored in.

There must be room for life's reality.

Events and living, breathing people can change direction, because there is nothing set in stone as a complete and unchangeable destiny or fate. But, because there is a preferred conclusion, your assigned guides and helpers will work very hard to nudge you toward your pre-life choices.

Adjustments are constantly being made, mindful of the most desirable outcome, the outcome that YOU picked. This life plan becomes a living entity, and the effect is a loving and beautiful work of art.

Jesse and I were at an important crossroads in these decisions, and we stood together on a platform above three very important choices.

I saw a representation of three potential bodies. They were draped in a covering of red, green and black, and atop each one lay a heavy gold medallion. Each of these neck pieces were of a different shape and design and there was a coordinating color of light that radiated deep within the middle of each one, offering a different choice of body type and life potentials.

The body was covered in this way as an example for me, and I was made to know that this was ONLY a representation created for my own understanding in this dream.

There is a general understanding during our time of choosing, of what the body will look like based on the genetic makeup, but more emphasis is placed on the bodies' potential to achieve the desired experience.

The particular facial looks of the body are not a concern to the soul who will embody it. There is no ego attached to being pretty or otherwise. Unless that is an element that will enhance the achievement of the end result, which is a successful learning experience for the soul.

I woke just as Jesse was making his selection, Black, and somehow this seemed no surprise to me. And although I do not recall what this color represented, I remember a feeling of, 'Oh boy, hold on,' and that we would both be having to step up our game, but also feeling much pride in his decision.

Trying Out a Life

subtle

(especially of a change or distinction) so delicate or precise as to be difficult to analyze or describe.

"This language expresses rich and subtle meanings"

fine, fine-drawn, ultra-fine, nice, overnice, minute, precise, narrow, tenuous; (of a mixture or effect) delicately complex and understated.

synonyms: understated, low-key, muted, toned down, subdued; making use of clever and indirect methods to achieve something.

"he tried a more subtle approach"

Last night I dreamed of a large Asian city, and I saw myself walking through the busy streets and shops. I was familiarizing myself with all of its nuances, looking for something, or rather being shown something. My night would be filled with examples and samples of possible lives I could live. I was investigating varying ways of life and who I was best suited to be for accomplishing a very special volunteer assignment. I was to assist in turning around or changing a specific course of the world.

I was trying on a role of a revolutionary, and I saw myself trying to evoke change by attending secret meetings and scratching words of opposition on political posters. I was recognized, caught, and imprisoned, and the Elders were not satisfied in what I could achieve this way. The role of a revolutionary did not suit my personality traits, and the desired goal would not be accomplished.

Soon after, I saw myself standing at the door of a studio watching beautiful young Asian women in dance attire. They were bending and turning about while using their hands to imitate a lovely flower. They were being schooled in the art of soft allure, and this training was for an entirely different approach to facilitate change.

They were called 'Subtles,' women who could do much to change the world by using more of a stealth technique. They were gifted in softening a closed or hardened mind, by implementing a non-threatening front of beauty and grace.

It was decided that my personality would adapt better to this role, and I was to join the Subtles. I wasn't disappointed with this choice and I agreed with the decision, but as I woke the thought ran through my mind, "Darn, I wanted to be a Geisha."

Interesting stuff comes through in dreams...

My take-away:

I will usually only report the facts of what I see, and leave out any commentary that has not been substantiated. But as I lay in bed after having the dream, thinking of what it all meant, I wanted to share 'the feeling' that was associated with this dream.

I was given an experimental, or rather a sample of possibilities of lives, and not remembering an actual past life, as I have spoken of before.

There is a big difference.

These snapshots do not include the chains of individual thoughts or memories of actually living the life. It is only an exploration into the possibilities of outcomes based on a soul's personal traits and attributes. A past life recall is as richly detailed as the life you are living right now. Again, there is a big difference.

This life would also be different because it was not a payment of a personal karmic debt or educational experience, but instead was a specific assignment. The outcome of my contribution was extremely important. I was a volunteer for this assignment, and the Spiritual Council was deeply involved in the decision-making process. They needed to find the right players for the roles to be played to obtain the objective.

I am not sure if I got the opportunity to live a life of a 'Subtle' because I have no memory of one, and have not had any further dreams or past life regression therapy to substantiate this one. But I found it very interesting to have gone through the examples and snapshots of these lives in this vivid dream, whether I was actually born and cultivated into being a Subtle woman in Asia or not.

Sister/Friend

As I worked to improve my 'hearing' skills, I used another ATV riding experience to talk to my sister Kaylyn, who now resides on the Other Side. The following conversation came as a surprise in its depth and information, and I admit I was a bit shocked in the discovery of how intermingled our lives have really been.

My husband and I were camping near Salida, Colorado, and a trip taken years earlier with an old friend was on my mind. One day as he paid me a compliment, he asked me if I had a sister. I laughed at the notion of it, and said "yes I do, and she is beautiful, but you wouldn't like her, she is on a fast track to becoming a bishop's wife, and not so much your type."

This statement represented the miles apart my sister and I were in our relationship. Though it had never suffered a formal break, we recognized that our mindsets were just too different to spend our free time together.

I knew her to be sweet and kind, but she was also closed minded, and to be honest, she was a bit too judgmental for my liking. I could feel her hold me at a distance and away from her, as I was too free with my emotions and too wild in her summation of my life. We spent many years in a sisterly way caring about one another, but without the gravy to give it more than just sustenance.

As I rode through the trees, I thought of my answer to Greg, when I heard her pipe into my head and say, "Well I did become a bishop's wife, didn't I?" I recognized her joking tone, and how she said it made me laugh out loud.

The connection was amazing. I could hear her, but not in an audible way. It was in the way of hearing your thoughts, except they were clearly not my own. My sister could hear my thoughts, and she could answer me with hers.

We talked for almost an hour that day, beginning with our family. The words she used were "Nothing Precedes a Family's Love."

I asked her about a lot of things including individual family members, most of which she wished not to speak of, saying "You already have the answers, and you should believe what is in your heart."

I asked her about the year before when she came to me through a medium. She had left me with a bombshell of a statement, saying "We were witches." the medium said Kaylyn had said this in a 'giggling' kind of way. I had been left to wonder about it, and I asked would she please help me understand what she meant.

She explained that we had shared a previous life together in a time of much mistrust in anything different from the norm. Religion was completely fear based, and many of the young ones were rebelling. She and I, and many of our friends had found strength in sharing new perspectives with each other, including the use of herbs for medicine.

She further explained that we did not like the power wielded by the preacher types, and were trying to offer new ideas and hope, and we had died because of it. I asked her how we died, and she said that details did not matter, but that some of us were hanged and some of us were burned.

She went on to say that it was a terrible time of fear and betrayal, as friends and family turned on each other to save themselves. Many of our dearest and trusted friends who had been less vocal about their discord with 'the ways' stepped back and away from us. Though they knew we had done nothing wrong, they held fast to the lies they had made up to divert attention from themselves, and from any association with 'us.'

She told me that this had a lot to do with the lives we chose this time. She decided to explore the part of the closed and judgmental mind, and I would hold onto my rebellion, determined to teach that you can have faith in a loving God, but also have an opened mind. She also told me that she had so much pride in me and my studies, and in my courage to share what I learn.

She began closing the connection by saying that we had both played our parts, that she had learned much from her experience this time around, and that I was to continue my quest. She added that there is much joy from those who know I am fulfilling my destiny. She encouraged me to keep going and I asked her how long I would be around here, and she teasingly laughed when she said, "awhile yet."

We were close to finishing when I thanked her for being my sister, and she immediately corrected me by saying "Sister/Friend," and I knew it was a perfect description of our roles together, and our eternal love for one another.

I am so grateful for this new understanding of 'us' and for the opportunity to know that there is so much more ahead than the roles we played here.

Lots of Me's

Although I have already been a witness to many of my previous lives, I am grateful for the continued teachings and the confirmation that came to me in a dream, in the form of a 'living photo' a few years ago.

I call it 'living' in the Harry Potter sense of pictures with motion and interaction, but not like a pre-recorded video. It's hard to find proper words to explain it, but the people in this representation were alive and in real time, and they were assembling themselves in a row to be seen by me as I lay in a dream state.

The photo was colored in a brown wash, like the carnival dress-up pictures that are made to look 'old time' and in the era of six shooters and saloons. This was the feeling the photo represented, and I watched some thirty people from various time periods stand shoulder to shoulder.

As my eyes perused this diverse group, I noted their varying styles of dress, and I focused on a handsome blonde man with a shield and bright gold breast plate over a finely pleated dress-like tunic. I had a feeling of deep trust in him, though I don't know why.

I saw the old black man that had stared back at me in a mirror in the middle of a dream.

I didn't get his name or much information about him, except that the me standing in front of the mirror was an entirely different me than the one looking back. The reflection revealed that I was of a different gender, age, and race.

In the era of the 30's, I was a little girl around two years old named Maddy. It was the time of the great dust bowl, and the air was not fit to breathe. Everything was covered in a fine powdery silt. Nothing would grow in my grandfather's fields, and I watched him wander outside wearing dirty overalls and a tired face. He looked so old, and he seemed to be watching for something to change or even a small sign of hope.

The large tree at the property line was nothing more now than a sun-bleached scarecrow. The branches looked like they were stretched out and reaching for something they could no longer get. The water that would not come had turned it into a sad reminder of what was no more.

There was a wagon sitting out front, but our horse no longer had the strength to pull it, even if we had someplace to go. The bones on his hips were trying to pop through his skin, and a dry sore was exposed to the dust and dirt.

This was the entirety of my world as seen through the screened door attached to the shack of a farmhouse. My time was spent watching my grandpapa, and I looked from field to tree, to horse to grandpa, and then back again and again. Even though I was only a small child, I knew there was much wrong in this world, and my mood was somber. I was plagued with coughing fits until I wet myself, and then I would cling incessantly to the hem of my mother's skirt for comfort.

The most familiar part of this life's memory was rubbing the worn cotton fabric of her skirt between my fingers and holding it against my face. It is something that I have carried to this lifetime, still finding a subconscious comfort in this act. Perhaps we do carry parts of our previous selves with us.

Now in this living portrait, my attention was drawn to one woman in particular as she did not seem the least bit invested or cooperative. She would stand almost sideways and looking away, while all the others faced me directly. This was her persona and she was true to it even still, or perhaps she was just acting in a familiar fashion to aide me in recognizing her quickly, and I did.

She was the one who looked back at me as a clear reflection while kneeling at the water's edge. Her hair was brown and curly, and she may have been deemed as plain looking because she seemed to have more teeth than her mouth could hold. But she was handsome enough to choose her lovers on her own terms, and then treat them in the most cavalier of ways. There was a lot more to her story, but in the end, I knew that her/my name was Tenna.

I saw Migella, the small boy/me who died at the soldier's hand, and so many other faces as they gathered together for the somber faced photo reflecting the photography style of the 1800's.

The film exposure of the times was a long and painstaking process, and a natural smile was impossible to hold for the extended time needed. A pose that could be held completely still was the optimal choice, and it was all being repeated for me in this representation and spiritual learning tool.

I regretted that I had not met all of them yet, and I tried to memorize each individual in hopes that one night, I might. Perhaps I will remember their/my story in a dream when it is deemed most beneficial for my spiritual progression. But for now, I will hold onto a memory of a picture, with the complete certainty that they were all of the characters and personalities who had been/were me.

Note: I am always so grateful for the teachings and special attention I receive that aides in my understanding and spiritual growth. I appreciate that it does not offend my guide or teachers when I ask for confirmation of what I see. They are happy to accommodate my need for assurance as I walk toward enlightenment, and they will nudge and prompt me along the way.

Because this is important information, I do not take its distribution lightly, and I share this personal knowledge with my whole heart and soul.

P.S. I would love to know the complete story of the girl dressed as a flapper, and of the beautiful Japanese woman wearing a white painted and powdered face, but so far I have not received any further details.

REINCARNATION SCENARIO:

Same Bush
Different Rose

The first time I heard the following song, it sent shivers down my spine. Feel free to place a bookmark here and Google this song, and prepare for goosebumps.

THE HIGHWAY MAN

written by Jimmy Webb

Willie Nelson:
I was a Highwayman, alone the coach roads I did ride
With a sword and pistol by my side
Many a young maid lost her babbles to my trade
Many a soldier shed his lifeblood to my trade
The bastards hung me in the spring of twenty-five
But I am still alive

Kris Kristofferson:
I was a sailor
I was born upon the tide
With the sea I did abide
I sailed a schooner around the horn to Mexico
I went aloft and furled the mainsail in a blow
And when the yards broke off they say that I got killed
But I am living still

Waylon Jennings:
I was a dam builder across the river deep and wide
Where steel and water did collide
A place called Boulder on the wild Colorado
I slipped and fell into the wet concrete below
They buried me in that great tomb that knows no sound
But I am still around
I'll always be around and around and around and around

Johnny Cash:
I fly a starship across the Universe divide
And when I reach the Other Side
I'll find a place to rest my spirit if I can
Perhaps I may become a Highwayman again
Or I may simply be a single drop of rain
But I will remain
And I'll be back again and again and again and again and again...

It's gonna be alright.

*Give yourself a moment of mindfulness. Be still now.
Turn down the volume
Of all the noise and chatter around you
And tune in to your inner voice
Your inner wisdom
And listen and follow your own instinct
And you will be alright.
Everything will be alright.*

- Claudia Watts Edge

9

Pause and Reflect

Life's Ride is Full of Carnival Balloons

Whoever said that "life is like a carnival" coined a good description of our time here on Earth.

In the early years of recognizing and recording my vivid dreams, the following was one of my first live and in color dream/experiences of Spirit School.

I was watching people going about their business as an everyday spectator on a busy street. The scene was vividly memorable because each person had a cluster of colored balloons floating above their head, and they were tied with string as if just purchased from a carnival vender. Needless to say, the vision was colorful fun, and I was excited that I could see what people had no idea was floating above them.

Soon, the teacher addressed me and asked if I would like to see my own balloons and I answered an enthusiastic "Yes!" But my enthusiasm quickly faded, as the balloons above my head looked entirely different. The strings were withered, hanging loose and holding only three droopy balloons.

One red balloon was still trying to reach for the heights, but was not full and taught, the air slowing slipping away. Another was drifting loosely on the floor, all but done, and the last one was completely pruned, having lost all of its virility. It had shrunk to the size of a wilted apple and was soft and pliable, but still tied to the lackluster bunch.

My scene seemed a sad reflection in comparison to all the others', and my reaction was immediate disappointment. A muffled chuckle was the reaction I got from my guide and teacher, as my eyes began to fill with tears, followed quickly by their "Ahh honey, this is a good thing, and you should be happy." But I saw nothing in this picture to smile about, and as my guide comforted me, the teacher explained, "Let me be clear little one, that this was just an illustration, and there are no balloons floating above your heads, but this seemed the easiest way to explain life's purpose."

He continued, "You are born into the world with certain INTENTIONS, and things you plan to conquer in your life. All expectations are placed by your own self and are of your own FREE WILL to complete. Your objectives are noted and there is nothing more than our happiness for you when you achieve them, and there is only understanding and love if your goals are not fully executed before you return."

I was trying to suppress my sniffles as he continued to explain, "The example of the full cascade of balloons represents a life still full of possibilities and achievements ahead, and the representation of the condition of your balloons means your mission is almost complete. You should take pride in the state of your balloons, because it means you have accomplished almost all of the intentions you set before your birth."

This representation has stayed with me, the colorful details etched into my mind so much that when my body seemed to be giving out last year before several surgeries, I confided to my husband that I knew my time here was winding down. But he was having none of it, and I woke the next morning to a vase of beautiful roses and a cluster of balloons hovering above it.

The image of the tight and lustrous colors was a happy sight, but within hours the red one was laying on the counter, and he quickly snatched it from the bunch hoping I hadn't noticed.

He continued to try to keep the bunch intact for several days, until one morning they were all removed. The job was impossible to keep up with, but I will always remember how thoughtful his intentions were, and that he would try so hard to personally change the inevitable for me.

Grandma, Are You Not Brave?

The first signs of spring are here. The air is warming and it's time to weed around the yellow daffodils popping up in the garden. It has been an extremely long winter and I am in need of a good dose of sunshine. I decided it was time to take my winter worn grandchildren to the nearby playground for some fun.

Harper and Jaydan are three-year-old twins and are just about the cutest little cherubs I have ever seen. I watch them climb, balance, and slide with proud grandma enthusiasm, as I clap and cheer each new accomplishment.

It was just about time to go home when Jaydan yelled from the top of the slide, asking will I please slide down together with him. I took a deep breath hoping for a blast of energy while looking for an easy entry. But this particular jungle gym would not be so accommodating; apparently you must earn your way to the top.

I had a choice of maneuvering the hand-to-foot rock wall climb aboard tiny plastic pegs, or swinging over the hand ring bridge. Oh, and my personal favorite, the uneven topsy-turvy lily pad things, that once you climb aboard, well, you better hang on because it's going to be a bumpy ride.

I was in no mood to break a hip, so I tried to turn down his sweet request by telling him that I was too big and too tired. But he was having none of my excuses, cutting my boo-hoos off in midsentence. He gave me a good long look before he said, "Grandma, are you not brave?"

After two surgeries in the past three months, I had been feeling all of my sixty plus years.

I've had two broken ankles at the same time, from (don't laugh) a gardening accident, that still limits and gives me pain after eight years. I've had a broken arm and elbow from a jogging incident causing me to drive 500 hundred miles with one hand in order to get myself home. And just yesterday, I had found that the pressure I felt in my right ear is nerve damage, and I'm losing some of my hearing.

I'm not asking for sympathy here, but Grandma is kind of falling apart. Jaydan's question both surprised and bothered me, and I began to build my defense. I have accepted the fatigue, grey hair and the weight gain that comes with age, but how do you tell such little people that their Grandma used to be so much more than the out of breath person they know now?

In my mind full of memories, I was an adventure seeker, a scuba diver and sky jumper. I loved riding the rapids in the Colorado mountains, even choosing to zip-line in the Salida canyons for my fifty-eighth birthday present. So the questioning of my bravery stung more than it should have, and I decided to tell them a bit more about their Grandmother.

They were very interested in the concept of jumping out of a perfectly good airplane, and being able to breathe under the water. I guess I was trying to instill a sense of adventure in them, and perhaps some pride about this old woman who stood before them now.

Eventually we turned towards home, and I made a point to bring out the pictures of me in mid-air and trailing a parachute behind me. We pored over pictures of their Grandpa and I in great underwater shots, while earning advanced deep-water certifications and rescue diver status. They were fascinated at the thought of these adventures, asking questions about why someone would want to go under the water, or jump so high in the air, and we spent a great deal of time in the hows and whys of it all.

Harper's interest was in the lady with the black hair, and I explained that she was me. I was the lady in the pictures before my hair went white. Now both of them stared intently at the beautiful brave lady in the pictures, turning back to look at me now with completely puzzled looks on their faces. They were obviously struggling with the concept of aging. These innocents looked back and forth so many times, I just had to laugh, conceding that, yes, I do look different now.

Out of the mouths of babes, Jaydan spoke first, "Grandma why are you not having black hair anymore? Followed by Harper's idea, "Can you make it be black again?" Haha I thought, I wish it were that easy my sweets.

I realized then, that one has little control over the memories others will carry of you after you are gone. The adventurous lady with the black hair doesn't really live here anymore. Although I do feel her from time to time, she is for me only now, and that is OK. I understand that as we spend valuable time together, my grandchildren will develop their own memories of who their Grandmother was.

My hope is that they will remember the grand love that I held for each and every one of them, and that my arms opened wide at the very sight of them. And perhaps they will recall that my white hair carried the faintest scent of lavender, and there was always a big happy smile for them on my wrinkly face.

Dance with Me

There is a song called 'Dance with Me' by the group 'Orleans' and to this day I can't hear it without a quick up-turn of the volume, and a full smile.

The timing was perfect on this sunny September morning. I turned on the radio to the words **"Dance with me.. I want to be** your partner... dance with me... the music is just starting... night is calling... and I am falling... dance with me..."**

I can feel the grin stretch across my face as I let the radio waves envelope me and open the memories of the dance partners I have had in my life. **"Dance with me..."** I recall the excitement of the invitation, the brightness in their eyes, and the warmth of their body as they led me to the floor.

What a happy time, as the extended hand offers its possibilities, and the heart-beats flutter as they work to match each other's rhythms in time and tune, **"I want to be your partner... can't you see..."**

I am taking a moment this morning, to pay homage to the ones who made my temperature rise and my heart skip a beat. The music reminds me, and I bask in the pleasure of memories of a time when the floor rose to meet our steps together. They were all important dances to me.

I was lucky enough to fall in love with three of them. The first was in a band and was always making music for others. We never got our chance to dance together, and after many dances, I married the other two.

Today I am still happily married to the latter of the three and the memory of the tilt of his head and the happy smile he wore as we danced, is the mortar that holds us together as our aging bodies begin to fall apart.

"Fantasy... could never be so giving... I feel free... I hope that you are willing... pick the beat up... and pick your feet up... dance with me..."

I am grateful for the memories I have stored within me of the best of times, and the happiness that I find when they are so easily accessed in the words of a song.

Moon Walks with Jude

I am sure that my grandson Jude is a typical nine-year-old, but I share a wonderment in the questions he asks. He is full of them, and I am happy to ponder and discuss possibilities in the answers.

Over the years we have developed a strong bond and a deeply-seated trust in one and other.

We devote a special time each month, a signal that is ours to explore as we share our understanding of the world while looking at the full moon.

We celebrate that round yellow circle in the sky as it shines down on our faces. We spend warm summer nights in a backyard tent letting the light of the moon peer through the zippered skylight. And we bundle up against the cold while walking through fallen leaves or crunchy evening snow. We carry flashlights and headlamps yielding safe passage in the darkness of empty streets or woods, taking time to stop and turn them off to sample the brightness of a full moon's unique light.

Our conversations flow without effort, and we laugh with simple ease at nine-year-old sillies. A stick becomes a sword to defend against the shadows, the rain gutter is a dungeon filled with captured villains, and we hide behind trees to evade the headlights of a passing car. We sing, run, and tell knock-knock jokes along our evening stroll.

He is sure his flashlight can cast a shadow on the moon or at least blaze a lighted trail deep into the darkened sky toward it. We discuss who might be living there or on the planets in the vastness of space. We call out the names of the stars we know, and we make up names for the ones we don't, and we talk of one day being able to travel there together.

Just as the sun rises and sets every day, we can count on the moon changing from a barely visible sliver of crescent light until it grows into a bright solid ball. All of this and more is ours every month, and that is the consistency I strive for now as a grandparent. It is a remarkable second chance to exercise the patience I lacked with my own sweet children. Unfortunately for most of us, patience is a gift acquired much later in life, and as I face the remaining years, I think about the legacy I will leave.

Recently I underwent a surgical procedure and was bed ridden for several weeks. My head was in a medical fog, and I had not noticed the changing days or the night sky for quite some time. Not until I got an evening phone call from Jude saying,

"Grandma I woke up and couldn't sleep, I went to the window to get my water and I saw 'our' moon. I went downstairs to ask daddy if I could please call and ask you to go the window so we can see it together like we always do, and he said yes. Can you see it Grandma?"

I felt so much joy in that moment, even as I had to hold myself to climb out of bed and walk to the window so both us could witness 'our' moon. It was worth the sore stitches, a fair trade for the confirmation that our friendship is real, built with the time spent together on a consistent basis, and mortared with lunar light.

There is no control over what events will turn into the golden memories of a child, what will be will be, and I am hopeful that Jude's life will be filled with many experiences and countless memories for him to hold onto.

I am comforted by the thought that long after I am gone, when he stops long enough to ponder the heavens above, he will think of me and our connection to each other, built over many moons, and he will be able to feel me there beside him as he looks up.

Deep-Diving Angel

I married an adventurer with a need to do anything he hasn't done before, wanting to learn its nuances until he is satisfied enough to cross it off his list. We hadn't been together very long when he won a trip from his employer to Puerto Rico, and he decided that scuba diving was the next big thing he wanted to learn. He informed me and that we needed to jump into classes and get certified before the trip the following month.

I was not so sure about scuba diving, and it wasn't on my bucket list. I was not an avid swimmer, but I did OK for a girl who could swim while holding her face out of the water so her mascara wouldn't run.

We were still very much in the 'honeymoon' stage of our marriage, and so I said yes after his argument that scuba diving required a 'buddy system.' The buddy is your side-by-side support and backup for a wonderful but dangerous sport, and he offered the question, *Did I really want someone else to be his buddy?* He made a good point because I had planned on being his buddy for a very long time, and I knew I had to come on aboard, so to speak.

The next few weeks were filled with swimming pools and scuba equipment. I spent a lot of time at the bottom of the pool learning that I could actually breathe under water while sounding a lot like Darth Vader.

During our dives, I learned to enjoy the ocean from an entirely different vantage point. Its powerful waves cresting at the shoreline was so different from the new discovery of the quiet and gentle pull of the current and its colorful occupants. Both versions offered so much to love about the sea.

I found myself proclaiming to anyone who would listen that I had found the place where God goes when he just needs some peace from everything else. There is no place to carry stress down there, and it rises to the surface in bubbles with each draw of condensed breath.

It is easy to get caught up in the wonderful freedom of floating/hovering/flying; it is a soft dance in the hypnotic drift of the water. You check on your buddy, and he checks on you, while watching the compass for direction, depth and how much precious air is left in the tank that is strapped to your back.

In a new diver certification, depth is restricted, and it wasn't long before my dive buddy was ready to push forward to new depths.

He'd been there done that, and he needed something new, and when we came home from Puerto Rico we headed straight to the dive shop for more instruction and the next level of certifications.

Advanced Diving opened up a world of depth options and commanded more respect and fewer restrictions from the dive-master who was busy minding the rest of the group. As an advanced diver you have experience, and are less likely to let yourself drift away or forget about vital check points. I would consider myself an inexperienced advanced diver; it was a recipe for trouble, and I found it.

We were diving off the coast of Catalina. It was cold water diving, and we were suited in layers, our bodies covered by thick six mil wetsuits from boots to hood, to hold in body heat. It didn't take much time in the water before I used the instructors secret to stay warm and pee in your wet suit, OK... ahh better.

The underwater world was amazing, it was thick with vegetation and schools of bright orange Garibaldi. I was introduced to the kelp forest, and I found warmth amongst the tall stocks of green as they waved back and forth with the surging surf.

I thought it a wonderland, and I was so excited for the next dive that would take us below 100 feet. It would be our Advanced Certification Deep Dive. It was to coincide with a wall dive, where you let the air out of your vest and slowly drop against the underwater canyon walls. I found that pushing off of the wall and floating weightlessly into the depths, was as close to a walk in outer space as you can get, and I loved every minute of it.

As you slowly drift ever downward, you can also feel the temperature drop. It's much darker and colder down there, and there is not as much to see, because the majority of marine life lives closer to the top where the sunlight and food reside. I was getting cold and ready to go back up, and I signaled to my buddy that I wanted to start the ascending process towards the top.

A deep dive requires you to surface slowly, with a safety stop at half the maximum distance. You must wait there for a few minutes at around 60 feet, and again just below the surface at 20 feet for another check point. You must be mindful to save enough air for these necessary lifesaving pauses before surfacing.

I added some air to my vest to rise, but I was having trouble regulating the air pressure in this unfamiliar rental equipment, and the buoyancy of the thick wetsuit I had never worn before. Soon I was bounding towards the surface like an escaping balloon.

I was in trouble, big trouble. I had lost the ability to halt my assent at the required resting point. I began to panic, which is a big no-no underwater because when you panic, you stop thinking clearly and you will usually drown. A truly experienced diver would have assessed that there was too much air in the vest and let some out. I looked toward my buddy who had been directly in front of me. I could now see him looking from side to side for me, but I was far above him by then, and helplessly out of control.

I kicked and screamed, but no one could hear me. In my fear I was doing nothing but leaving a field of white bubbles behind me, and not a sound that anyone else could hear.

There was a point of no return, and I had reached it. Going directly to the top is one sure way of killing a diver. The body's tissues are full of nitrogen that will cause decompression sickness or a lung embolism. It is an excruciating death, or at the very least a lengthy stint in a hospital's decompression oxygen chambers, with a possibility of blindness and severe lung damage.

This was not to be my fate, as I suddenly felt a firm hand grab ahold of my ankle, and I was physically stopped dead in the water, pun intended. I had assumed that my husband had seen my distress and caught up to me, but he told me that when he couldn't see me, he thought it wise to back track and look for me before he surfaced. He was upset at being separated, and he had no idea of my ordeal. I asked the instructor, and again later on the dive boat, who I could thank for grabbing me, but it seemed that no one in my group had been my rescuer. I was left with the question of who had saved me that day.

So many years later, and after learning how to communicate with my spirit guide, this was one of my many questions, had there been an intervention in the water from the Other Side?

I was answered in the way that we have worked out together for my best understanding. It was a resounding "Yes," that I had indeed been saved by a heavenly hand.

Later that night I received another confirmation of this in a dream, viewing the situation from an outside perspective. I saw myself rising away from the others, as panic and fear took over my actions. I then saw a hand extend from a brown robe, reaching out from the depths to take hold of me. It was the strong and yet gentle hand that I will forever know is there to help and guide me, even when I cannot see it.

I had originally ended the story here, but because I had been guided to write it, I spent time revisiting it in my journal, and I was given a feeling of confirmation that indeed, the angels do protect us from harm, especially when you have much left to do on the road ahead in your lifetime.

It seems such a waste to die early, and I am not speaking in terms of age, as one can accomplish specific goals in a short time. But I speak of dying without accomplishing what you had set out to do, and then having to come back and repeat all of the groundwork again. It just doesn't make sense to me to get to the same position, in order to accomplish what you set out to do in the first place.

The protective white light makes sense to me, enveloping us in safety. Could it be that the fumbling of car keys or the extra-long stop light that delays us, is an intentional safety stop as well?

I have often heard that these types of delays are used to keep us out of harm's way and out of an accident that will happen in mere seconds. We hear the survivor's claim, "If I had been 10 feet closer, or a minute earlier," or, "for some reason I turned left instead of right," and the famous "I don't know why I changed my seat at the last moment."

Perhaps Jesse's Vikingism is correct, that "If it is your day to die, then it is a good day to die, and if it is your time to die, then do it doing something you love." It seems an opportunity to quit worrying about the 'when' then doesn't it? And perhaps it's an invitation to live your life to the fullest.

Once you have achieved the mysterious goal you have no memory of setting, you are also near the end of your estimated time to be here. Your carnival balloons are limp and pruning, and the angels' light of protection is lifted, or at least eased off, so that you are now vulnerable to life's risks and probabilities, and soon enough your soul will be back home. Could it be then that it is pretty near impossible for our Earth-selves to fight heaven and the soul clock?

My mother spoke of the contract she made with my father, and the understanding that he was to exit early, as a catalyst for me and the other members of the family. It definitely put us on a completely different path of experience, and one that we would never have chosen on our own volition. It forced us into different roles and opportunities. We had all felt so perfect in the family bubble he had created for us, but now the bubble was popped, and we were to be whisked into the winds of change.

Earth Claudia has questioned his seemingly short life, but it seems that it was meant to be exactly that, and although I do not have all the answers, I am grateful for the events and the follow-up dreams that help me connect some of the dots.

Did You Realize
We Have Been Talking for 11 Minutes?

A phone call came from my grandson Jude; he wanted to invite me to school lunch at the special birthday table. It was an honor to be asked, and of course I said I would be there.

He spent the next few minutes reciting the school rules, and the precise time I needed to arrive. "Make sure your there at exactly 11:55 Grandma," and I promised that I would be there at the appointed time.

The conversation continued as we decided on what I would bring for our lunch, and then he blurted out in mid-sentence, "Did you realize we have been talking for 11 minutes, and we're still talking?" I asked him if he felt like we had talked long enough, and I could tell by his polite pause, that perhaps we had. I offered him an out by saying that we could save anything we still wanted to talk about until tomorrow. It was a deal.

Later that day I sat down in front of the wall calendar, with pictures and scenes depicting the seasons. I still enjoy using this paper form to view my upcoming schedule. I was working within the theory of having an entire month of time to use, as I pulled out a marker and blocked out the days and the times of my 'unavailability.' I set post-it notes on the side full of approaching birthdays and appointments that need to be made, or kept.

It was then that I noticed how few days and times we allocate for ourselves, the times in between busy work schedules and other 'have to do's.' Our lives charge ahead minute by minute, as a fragile infrastructure is built on fragmented moments that we string together. All of them are important, all are necessary, though we hang onto and remember very few of them.

I am old enough now to celebrate the new minutes that come with the start of each new day, though I regret that I am often careless with them, tossing them to the wind before I have even taken notice of them.

Jude noticed them, and he was adding them up as they fled by, while I was consumed by our conversation. To a little boy, 11 minutes can seem like an eternity when there is so much else to do and learn.

I appreciated his honesty with me, and the lesson of the fragility of minutes, and though I don't have as many left as I would like to, I am happy to share a grouping of an entire 11 of them, anytime he can spare them.

Press Pause and Reflect

When you find yourself
in a new situation
a new circumstance
a new life experience
everything that requires healing
is going to rush to the surface

And if you don't take a minute
to breathe
to gather yourself
to pray

you will do
what you've always done

So...
you've got to be clear enough
grounded enough
centered enough
to say
how am I going to handle it this time
The lesson is
take a pause

We go from being 20 to 30
without a pause
30 to 40 without a pause
We go from one job to the next
from one bed to the next
without a pause
Pause boo
and take a breath

- Iyanla Vanzant

My Resolve

On this beautiful Sunday afternoon, all was well as I was coming to the completion of 'setting' this book's chapters, story lines, and headings. Everything was making sense and falling into place, as if I were receiving 'help,' and you already know that I more than believe this to be fact.

So, what happened today, you might ask, and I can tell you it was not a pretty picture. A careless key stroke sent waves of confusion into myself and my computer. It did what I confirmed it should do, "Do you want to replace this with what already exists in this file?" But I was careless in my response, and weeks of hard work were replaced with something unintentional and unimportant, and much of the book was gone.

I spent hours in devastated tears, but found that all was not lost. It was just a setback to lose so much time and to have to retype stories that had already been completed and edited. I called out for help, "Please help me find the way to fix this." I lay in my bed in the middle of the afternoon, unrepentantly wasting time in a downward spiral of depression. It was my due, and I can cry if I want to.

I'm tired, I have been on a fast track to finish, perhaps too tired to write today, but it is my 'Sunday free day' and a time I allow myself to write and accomplish much. I heard the word '*RESOLVE*' through my tears, and I shushed it away, talking back to it, **"Please, I don't want a lesson right now, I am so not in the mood!"** But I heard it again, "*Is this your resolve?*" and I spit back an answer:

"Why are you questioning my resolve now after so many months of climbing out of bed in the middle of the night, or waking up in the early hours of the morning to write this book, the one that 'YOU' asked for? Am I not proving my 'RESOLVE' to you? Don't you know that I am going to finish this?"

And the answer came back in a tone that proved slow and wise, *"Oh but I do know that you will finish, I was just making sure that you knew it too."*

Jeff's Star

I wanted to write of the personality differences that make up the sum total of a family; each member, each sibling an original. Most of us have questioned how there can be so much difference between each other when we came from the same gene pool. But we are born with our own roles to play and a preplanned agenda, and the blood line has very little to do with it.

The following dream/experience is written for my brother Jeff. I am the oldest of five, he being the next in line, and with barely 15 months between us, we have shared a lot of growing up together.

Last night I was happy to be attending Spirit School again, and I was being shown the true nature of the stars. This lesson surrounded itself within a confirmation of my memory of the tunnel I traveled in, during my Earth death. The tunnel was made of stars, each stretching out to show an array of fiery colors as I passed by. I love the movie 'CONTACT' with Jodie Foster, as it reminds me of my own tunnel travel.

As each star grew closer, I could hear it speak to me, offering love and acceptance, best wishes and many, many welcomes. It was a wonderful experience to witness that the stars are alive and intelligent, with distinct personalities.

Anyway, back to the dream experience, and its short but powerful lesson.

November 23, 2015

As I stood in the dark with my trusted Spirit Teacher, he asked if I wanted to see 'Jeff's Star.' "Of course!" I said, as I raised my gaze toward the vast expanse of sky.

At that moment, one particular star twinkled at me, and it seemed to be puffing itself up to be noticed. I immediately recognized my body building and forever oiled and tanned brother's personality in this act of pageantry.

I will not offer any opinion here on what or who the stars really are. Are they us? I do not know, or I cannot remember. I do not have enough information to answer those questions in full confidence. But what I do know for sure, is that last night I was shown my brother Jeff's Star, and it was beautiful.

The Heavens do not Disappoint!

This dream/vision was received in the nick of time, and is being added at the last possible moment, AFTER the book layout. This a big deal because it moves all of the pages, and headings and chapters and pictures and coordinating page numbers, and everything is thrown out of whack. But I cannot listen to the no's, and the reasons why I am getting pushback to add this caveat to a 'finished' story.

All I know is this lovely vision is important, and because it was given to me 'in time' or at least before printing, I must share it here. Thank you, John Melody for making it all work out.

I lay in restful darkness not yet asleep, though my eyes were closed, when a large screen appeared in front of me. It was filled with many faces floating in the air in front of me and all were surrounded in black. There were hundreds of these renderings. The way their heads rested atop their shoulders reminded me of chess pieces, and they filled the entirety of the expanse of my vision.

Each face was so different from the others, a perfect capture of gender, race, color and age. I looked to see if any of these faces looked familiar to me, but as I tried to focus and distinguish one from another, the entire field changed. The faces were replaced... WITH STARS... billions of brilliant sparkling points of light. I was looking into the night sky and the stars that reside there.

I was looking at you and me, and all of us were holding our own place in the vastness of space and time.

It was a remarkable WOW moment for me, and I was in absolute awe of what I had just witnessed. I have contemplated it for many days now, still not fully comprehending the complexity of what this can possibly mean. But I offer it here to you dear reader, because after being asked by my trusted guide if I would like to see my brother Jeff's star, I have some good ideas.

I have used this expression before, and it seems to fit perfectly right here" "I am sure of what I know, and I'm sure there is so much more that I don't."

"My path is not new age, in fact, it is quite ancient"

- Claudia Edge

10

A Change Is Gonna Come

The world is alive and vital.

On July 25, 2013, during a vision of icy pyramid-looking structures in the Antarctic, I received this message:

Much will be discovered as the ice melts...

These words came to me in the early morning of June 2, 2014:

The world is alive and vital.
There is a great deal coming in changes of borders and in rulers.
Be at peace with your inner knowing.

The Twelve Apostles

Recently I had a dream that tied into a prophetic dream I had several years ago.

The first dream showed a change coming to the world, and a clear ability to 'see' each other's true selves. It was shown as a brightly colored representation of our spiritual progression, and how beautiful colors will encompass us, attaching and becoming a part of us.

Perhaps this is the Aura that we have heard about in new age speak, but in the changing world, ALL OF US will be able to see it. It will make it very easy to see the 'truth' of a person and their motivations. Generosity and kindness will be reflected in light-hearted colors, the greens of healers, or a muddled and musty darkness will warn of deceit.

A darkened persona will represent one holding greed and untruths, and their dark or blackened aura will be the first thing you will notice. There will be no hiding from it; you either hold the light and colors within, or you do not.

This will be an easy and universal way of recognizing the entirety of who we are, and no longer will one be fooled by the silver-tongued, with a false story or explanation of wrong-doing. If you are self-serving and a teller of untruths, you will be easily recognized for it.

I saw that in the state of our true colors being shown, a trusting and open society arose as the result. Our relationships blossomed, including relationships with the government, and with those holding office.

Intent was clearly seen, and we grew together in Peace and Prosperity.

So, now to the most recent teaching dream....

I was in great angst. Someone was accusing me of an act that I did not commit. I wanted to shout from the rooftops and proclaim my innocence, that I did not do this thing of which I was being accused.

A court date was chosen; the accuser would have a chance to tell his story in hopes of financial gain, and I would have the opportunity to defend myself.

The day arrived, and I took my place opposite my accuser. He stood ready to testify against me, but before he was asked to speak, a large group of men proceeded into the courtroom causing a considerable stir. They each wore a long white linen tunic, suggesting the biblical attire of long ago, but they were also clean shaven and their haircuts were modern. A hush fell over the courtroom as they quietly took their seats.

It was a breathtaking moment, because it felt as if both greatness and reverence had arrived, and an onlooker near me whispered, "The 12 Apostles are here."

They never uttered a word, as they were not there to take part in the proceedings or to pass judgement in any way. They came only to witness and observe.

The judge gestured toward the accuser to state his case, but the silence continued as the accuser seemed to be struggling to form the words. He was actively moving his hands at his throat and lips. His mouth was open, but his tongue could only curl from side to side, and he was unable to roll out his untruthful story.

The courtroom audience watched in earnest as he struggled, until he finally gave up and gathered his papers of false evidence and accusations. He left with his head hung in shame. He could not bring himself to lie; it was physically impossible to do in the presence of these twelve men. I was elated as the case against me was dismissed, and then I woke up.

As I lay in the dark, I wondered about who the twelve Apostles really were. *Apostle* is a word I had heard in my youth in Sunday school, but there was a significance in their arrival in my dream as a group of twelve. I Googled 'the twelve Apostles' and I was right in my assessment that they were, *'those who walked with Jesus as he taught the masses.'*

I am grateful for these vivid teaching dreams.

They have shown me that there is a time coming when the Earth will know peace, and that we will all prosper as we show each other kindness and learn to speak only in truths. I have been shown the possibilities of this world and its beauty, and I know that it is both possible, and on its way to fruition.

Mastodons and Flying Machines

September 24, 2016

While vividly dreaming, I found myself standing in a ravine between two mountain cliffs. I was looking at a bush as tall as a tree at the dry creek's edge, and I marveled at its vivid pink feathery splendor. I had never seen anything like this plant before, the foliage was so lush and wispy, and each airy blade came straight up from the ground in a grouping that fanned out and reached towards the sky. The plumes were strong, yet pliable enough to move softly in the breeze.

My attention was suddenly drawn to the top of the mountain, and above me I heard a deep roar echo through the canyon. A huge animal was standing at the cliff's edge. It had massive tusks, and a trunk that it was raising and lowering in a formal show of power, and a word came to mind: *Mastodon*.

I watched this animal from a time of long ago as it stomped about, and then suddenly the canyon began to change. Water was filling the creek bed and I quickly made my way up to its dry edge. What was once a sandy ravine was now a flowing river, and the pink bushes had adapted to their new environment. They were still beautiful and vibrant, but they were swaying with the motion of the water now.

I was surprised when I saw a type of ship in the sky. It was moving very slowly, and with no sound of an engine. It began to fly very low and directly over the gully, and I watched it slowly lower itself into the water.

This ship was so large that it looked completely out of place here in this natural setting.

I continued to watch it closely through the camouflage of pink, its single red headlight now shown under the water. It moved like a type of flying submarine, smoothly maneuvering its way downriver until it reached an entrance to a cave or underworld...

It was a very telling scene, and I could not get it out of my mind. I felt I had been witness to a story of beginnings... the early years of Earth marked by seeing a Mastodon.

Was this observation the mark of the very beginnings of life as viewed by peering through this marvelous species of plant and animal life that are both no longer here?

And perhaps the mark of an intelligent life form that still resides in the depths of our unknown waters?

New Earth Second Earth

June 27, 2015

Last night I dreamed as I have many times since childhood, of the coming of the second planet.

In my dreams I am standing alone as I watch it slide into view. It is alive and in motion, and it situates itself in the sky. Its movement is slow and deliberate, as it postures between the moon and the familiar ground I stand upon. It is a beautiful blue and green ball, and I marvel at its perfection as it eases into its own place in the sky.

When it finally settled, an energy began to emanate from it appearing as a mist or vapor, and I was made to know that the mist was intelligent. It settled on either side of me, eventually surrounding me, but I was not afraid. It would be selective as it traveled the Earth, finding those who were ready to advance.

The time had come and a transformation was taking place, and unfortunately there were those who were not yet ready. This change is not a judgment of righteousness or a punishment as many of us have been taught. It is simply the dimensional change and advancement that the Earth has earned, and of our ability to adapt to its new and higher vibration.

No longer would we be trapped in the heavy and sluggish third dimension; we would be advancing to the fifth. This will require a physical transformation, and it is only possible for those who are already in the process of letting go of fear and uncertainty, and are practicing acceptance and love.

There is complete certainty to be had, but only if one can open one's self to it. Many will perish from this world, leaving their physical selves behind, thus freeing the spirit to go on. It will be free to learn and to continue karmic lessons, or whatever else must be done to complete themselves in the spiritual, so they can continue to move forward. NO ONE IS LOST, ALL ARE OF GOD.

This visual of another planet is not new to me. I have seen it many times before, appearing and then sliding itself into a position above us all. I do not know when it will happen, but I offer my own certainty that it will come. Scientific studies are showing the possibility of another Earth-like planet that they feel is near but haven't seen yet. I can only offer what my dreams and visions show and tell me, and I give no personal speculation or opinion other than what I am shown or told. But I must report seeing the coming of a beautiful new world, filled with beautiful new and loving humans.

Months later I woke from another dream of the New Earth and the blue and green ball coming into view. It is so beautiful, and it is on its way.

Black Crystal Healing Chambers

I found myself in Spirit School again, the wonderful place I am allowed to attend in my dreams. I am introduced to new concepts and ideas in the most loving and positive learning environment, and with the most patient of teachers. The class is usually held in nature, and last night I found myself walking across a beach away from the shoreline, and toward large standing rock formations. I walked, circling around them while running my hands across them, and found that each one stood separately.

Each rock contained a hole that was large enough to climb into, but it wasn't scary like a tunnel or a cave. The inside of the chamber was made entirely of crystals, and they were as black as coal, but not dirty like coal can be. The hole was just below ground level, and it was carved out enough to be able to climb in and sit. It was a little tight, but not uncomfortable, and it reminded me of the old stereo chairs of the 1970's, where there was no need for a headset or ear buds to listen because the chair itself was the speaker, and you were surrounded in a comfortable musical chamber.

This was a 'whole' as I called it (not hole) and I was made to understand this 'whole' was a 'Healing Energy Chamber.' My teacher had given me an ecstatic "CORRECT!" seeming very pleased with my attention to detail when I said, "This 'whole' has an entirely different vibration than the last one."

I wanted to know more. "Was this an energy source or a portal?" Each rock formation held a different energy vibration. Did they each go to a different place in the Universe? Or did they target a specific area of the body that needed healing or repair? My mind was so full of questions, and I was disappointed to wake without remembering all the answers, but I did wake carrying a word on my lips, CRINETIC REPORT, and I had to search Google for the meaning: *crystalline rocks*. I found myself reading geologist reports of crystals created in different periods during Earth's development. I know and understand that there is power in crystals, and I am sure that one day we will discover and harness this power for healing, regeneration, and limitless technologies of travel and energy sources.

Within a day of this dream I was drawn to read a report by the Epoch Times. It came from someone in a Facebook group, and now it is magically placed in front of my face. Again, serendipity at work.

The article was called, *They're Alive! Megalithic Sites are More Than Just Stones*, dated 11/2/16 and based on the book by Freddy Silva, *The Divine Blueprint: Temples, Power Places, and The Global Plan to Shape the Human Soul*.

A Change Is Gonna Come | 173

I am constantly in awe of what I am shown, and the efforts given to confirm my dreams and to help me understand their meaning.

For further research, also look into telluric currents, megalithic structures, or magnetite crystals.

The Place of Universal Knowledge

A few years ago, in deep meditation, I had a vision rich in detail and information. I saw a spiral in front of me, spinning with a soft yet enticing pull that felt like an invitation to enter.

I found myself in space, or rather in *a* space, and I knew it to be The Place of Universal Knowledge.

New technology was floating all around me there. I recognized some things, but there was so much that I did not. There were many different shapes of gadgets and things we could only imagine in science fiction. I saw a checkerboard that I have seen many times before in my dreams, and I recognized a long titanium beam that was being used to build a grid system. I knew this, because I had previously dreamed of moving a similar metal beam with nothing more than thought. I am at a loss to explain how I could do this or why. Earth's protection perhaps? I say this because I remembered viewing the Earth below me as I eased the beam along with my mind and docked it into place.

I saw squares the size of cell phones, but they were somehow different and so much more advanced than the miracles we hold now. I saw written formulas having no idea of what they meant other than valuable solutions to equations that floated there amongst everything else. I noticed really small micro-chip kinds of things in this space, where there is an abundance of wonder in technological advancements, just waiting to be discovered by someone with a readied mind to understand and replicate it when awake. We are assisted with these big ideas, not because we can't do it on our own, because these ideas come from our own higher consciousness levels.

The mathematics, formulas, and the projects themselves are examples of how it will work. We get to see a brief glimpse of these ideas in our unconscious states of sleep, and we wake with a thought of it, a small piece to comprehend and research, to study and work on, with a place to start from.

Nicola Tesla understood this way to new ideas, and he acknowledged and gave gratitude for the information he received. He became quite adept at retrieving information this way, and at the time he mentioned extraterrestrials and the ability to hear transmissions from other worlds. This could very well be, but I also believe it came from his own subconscious, as we are all brilliant in this state.

There was so much more to his work that has never been fully realized. All of his notes and journals were confiscated upon his death, but what he had access to, so does another. The world waits for the next Einstein or Tesla in like-mind to access all that is waiting there.

My visit to The Place of Universal Knowledge was an amazing journey, and I am grateful to have been lucid enough to remember it. It is real, and it exists easily within our reach. We have all visited it in our unconscious state of mind, as it waits for the future's brilliant ones to dream their way into the spiral and exit with so much to share with the world.

> *My brain is only a receiver.*
> *In the Universe there is*
> *a core from which we can obtain*
> *Knowledge Strength and Inspiration.*
> *I've not penetrated into the secrets of this core*
> *but I know that it exists.*

- Nicola Tesla

Some Things Are Set

I have written before of the gift of our free will, but I want to clarify one of its points, because I was taught that some things that are unchangeable. Let me explain by sharing the dream/experience that was used as a teaching tool for my understanding.

I was to live through a kind of Groundhog Day movie, the same start every morning, to relive a day that would result in a horrible explosion. My participation varied as I tried to save the day and tweak the ending. But the result was always the same, and only the circumstances that had caused it were changed. I tried everything, but even switching the location did not help. Each time the outcome was inevitably the same.

In some instances, I would go to the authorities to enlist help, but would only succeed in making myself a suspect. How did I know so much before this thing actually happened? And why was I so obsessed about a lit match, a placement of shoes, or who was near a boat in this repeating drama? Over and over again the scene was set up so I could change my approach and tactics. What looked like an opportunity to stop the event would only alter its course, but not enough to keep it from happening. I was unable to stop it, no matter how many chances I was given to try.

I woke up knowing that I had been taught another spiritual lesson, and that there are certain situations and events that are supposed to take place. No matter how hard we try to prevent them, or how horrible they seem to be. Though it is hard to accept and understand, some seemingly bad things are supposed to happen. Even in the knowing that some people will die, they have contracted to do so in this pre-planned event that is structured as a catalyst for future change.

My take-away from this angst-filled experience is to live and enjoy life, and to not live in fear of the possibilities of what can happen.

Because if it is supposed to happen, it will happen. Instead listen, pay attention, take part in your life and do your best with every day.

Some outcomes are going to happen because they are meant to, and then you must deal with the aftermath and its consequences as best you can. This is cause and effect, and there are lessons and opportunities to be gained from these so-called accidents, because they are purposely SET TO HAPPEN so we may experience the lesson they bring.

Paper Mache

I had a dream labeled METAPHOR, and it was given to help me understand the changes that were to come to the Earth and to those of us living on it.

I was standing in an open field of green, groomed grass, like a soccer field. I was having a simple conversation with several ladies when I noticed a very tall woman walking toward us. Someone was guiding her arm as she took small, careful steps.

As she got closer, I could see why she needed help—her head was large and made completely out of paper mache, strips of paper and glue. It was white and rough, and I saw only empty holes where her eyes and ears should have been. There was nothing else inside of this paper mache head.

The entire group had stopped talking when they noticed her, and now we were in a hushed awe as she stopped directly in front of us. Somehow she knew that we were there, but how could she know without being able to see or hear us? We peeked inquisitively into her seemingly empty head.

She addressed us quite eloquently, telling us not to feel sorry for her, because she was going through 'a change.' She was not at all unhappy in what she had lost. Instead she was very excited about what she was to receive in its place. All was under construction for now, but soon...

I woke up knowing that I had been given a vivid example of what will be taking place in all of us, as the change for the new world is readied. We must understand that we should not be upset about what will be lost, because it is necessary to be cleared away and made anew, and we are about to receive so much more!

The Big Wave

October 15, 2015

Lately when a message is given, it comes as soon as I sit down to relax or close my eyes. It is as if the download of information is just poised and ready for my attention. It is accompanied by a visual for clarity, or at least to provoke further thought and questions.

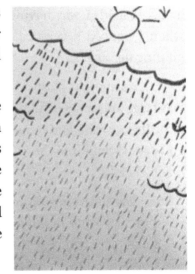

I see a white screen, letting me know to prepare myself, and then a moving picture appears on it. Sometimes it is over within seconds, but those seconds are so very powerful. They leave me with an indelible impression, and a question of what I am to do with the information.

I have written of the world change that is coming, and a feeling accentuated this vision. I saw a type of triangle filled with short lines, or what I call dashes. In the past a dash has referenced a person or people, and I will continue to use this reference.

There were so many dashes, and the triangle grew endlessly wider at the bottom, representing the billions of souls here on Earth. A large ball of white-gold light came into view, as if the sun were en route to hang closely over the Earth.

A flash of light came from within the ball, creating a wave that began to slowly ripple over the beginning rows of people-dashes. As the light moved over them, the color of the dashes grew deeper, thicker, and more pronounced. The wave continued immersing each dash with its light, row after row of dashes. None was left out; all were being touched by this directed light. When it was over, the ball of light began to retract backwards in the sky, and then the vision ended.

I include this story and my crude drawing of it here, in hopes it will assist in your own understanding. When the change comes, the light will find you, no matter where you are, or who you are. There will be no hiding from it, and you will be illuminated by its light. So set aside your fears, and face the beauty of that which is coming.

Looking into the Crater

As I was completing this book, I knew there were a few more stories that needed to be included, because it was shown to me in a dream using actual words. I watched as the curser moved across the page and left a clear message: 'KEEP SOME SPACES OPEN.'

I have been going through my journals for what I needed to include, and this one popped out to me. So, here goes... hang on...

September 23, 2016

For almost a year I have been seeing space when I close my eyes for sleep. The stars are gently moving in a soft rotating formation, like timed photography. This time I was camping and completely relaxed as I lay in a hammock, and I had just barely closed my eyes when the stars flashed before them.

I witnessed a multitude of bright shining stars, thousands of them arching clockwise, moving and alive. I wanted to enter this beautiful scene, to jump into the rotation. I felt like a kid in grade school waiting to gain entry into double-dutch rope-jumping as I was watched for the perfect moment to join and participate.

The scene lasted longer than it ever had before, and I strained my eyes, trying to bring it closer to me. Soon the stars began to meld and form a funnel. I wanted to jump in and I guess I must have, because now I was keeping up with the rotation. I was a part of it. I had a thought to concentrate on just one of the stars. It became brighter and larger and soon I found myself in front of it. It was a large ball, "A PLANET!" was my conscious thought, and as the scene continued, I thought, "It's not going away, I am here in front of a planet!"

It looked like the moon, grey, dusty and barren looking, Then I noticed three black craters close together, like the holes of a bowling ball, and I moved myself near the edge of one to peek inside.

What I saw was... hollow... it was hollow inside... it was not a solid ball of dirt and rock, but a huge active world of city structures. There were sleek black ships flying all around them, but they did not look strange or alien, sincerely, they could have been ours. But there were so many of them, hundreds flying about in an organized chaos. I then saw shards of sparks come from deep within the planet, set off by fireworks, all around the ships. The ships were no longer coming in; now they were all trying to go out, as more and more of the sparks filled the air around them.

I do not know for sure if this was for defense, or war, or a natural occurrence within the planet, like a volcano or something like that. I honestly do not know, nor will I speculate here, but I was anxious to pull away from the scene, easing backwards until I had a visual of the entire planet, and I thought aloud, "Was this our Moon?"

The scene changed, and I was floating above... now get this... 'The Face,' like the one seen on May 2001 from NASA's Mars Global Surveyor. But it was more of a full body structure, and it was awesome! This was no natural formation as NASA and the like would explain away as just another Martian mesa with unusual shadowing. It was constructed and purposeful, and I was seeing it as a metal formation in its shiny beginnings, long before it was covered by eons of space dust. I was standing next to it, the size of an ant compared to it, touching and marveling at its magnificence.

IT IS REAL! AND IT WAS MADE ON PURPOSE! I do not have answers about what its purpose is, or about who constructed it or how. But I am so deeply humbled to have been shown this in person, so to speak, and while completely awake. The experience gifted me an understanding of so much that we don't know is going on 'Out There.'

I am only reporting what I was shown without the benefit of knowing if this is a future event, or a glimpse into something historical. I cannot say for sure if I witnessed our moon or another planet's moon, or if the face I saw was on Mars or a similar planet. But I hold firm on what I was made to understand, and that is... a lot more going on beyond our world than we are led to believe, and I am going to keep my mind open and my eyes to the stars.

If you are asking questions
Of the universe
And are not receiving answers,
Ask better questions.

- Claudia Watts Edge

Please

As I was pulling into work, I was following this car. The sign in the back window says, "Learning stick sorry for any delay."

Knowing this information, I was very patient with their slow shifting, and honestly they were doing pretty well for still learning. Then I asked myself a tough question: Would I have been just as patient if the sign hadn't been there? I can almost definitely say no.

We don't know what someone is going through. We don't wear signs that illustrate our personal struggles. You don't see signs taped to people's shirts that say, "Going through a divorce", or "Lost a child", or "Feeling depressed", or "Diagnosed with cancer".

If we could read visually what those around us are going through we would definitely be nicer. But we shouldn't have to see signs and have reasons to treat strangers with kindness. We should do it anyway, whether we know what is going on or not. Whether they deserve it or not.

Read

11

Soft Speak

*"Never Look Down on Someone
Unless You Are Admiring Their Shoes"*

She Just Needed to Be Heard

Years ago, as a stressed-out young mother of five, I could easily find myself in confrontations with other drivers. I could yell obscenities with the best of them. I would focus my wrath toward the rude, thoughtless or just plain dumb drivers, who drove too slow or too close, didn't use a turn signal, or made rapidly swooping lane changes... I'm sure you get my drift.

It took many years and miles to learn that it does no one any good to yell at or flip off another driver. It always ends up escalating the situation, as well as one's blood pressure. It has taken a lot of practice to stay calm in these situations, though I can still find myself rolling my eyes and cursing under my breath at times.

Pulling up beside the offending driver at a stop light used to be a perfect place to display a full lashing and gnashing of teeth, but I have learned now that it is better not to engage and to just look full-on, straight forward. This leaves the opposing driver in an awkward state of confusion, flustered with the inability to share their own brilliant words and signs of equal contempt.

Now in my sixties, I have found that (sometimes), I can be the root of a road problem. I don't see as sharply as I used to, and because I am a realtor, I drive a little slower as I map out neighborhoods. Oh, how unfair age can be, because I have so enjoyed always being in the right. And I had tightly held on to righteous indignation that I was and had always been a perfect driver.

A few years ago, I detoured my drive home to pick up some take-out food. My engine idled away as the line and the wait grew really long. The alley to the speaker box and the serving window was narrow and in-between two buildings. With nowhere to go, there was nothing else to do but turn up the radio and wait.

The errand had started in the early stages of twilight, but now the skies had become dark. Night had set in, and I was back on the road trying to drive while managing two oversized cups and dinner on the passenger seat, leaving little attention to spare for the road in front of me.

The highway near my home was in a newer area, and streetlights were scarce. The road was long and straight, and the lack of traffic enabled me to drive quickly and freely. I was eager to get home before dinner was cold, and I took advantage of the solitary stretches between stop lights, when a car made a sudden right turn onto the road. It was directly in front of me, and I slammed on my brakes and pulled a rapid lane change as all of my dinner spilled to the floorboards. What an idiot! They could have killed us both! Why had they been in such a hurry to enter the straightaway, and why, directly in front of me?

I was proud of my quick defensive maneuvers, while managing to hold down and blare my horn indignantly for a good 30 seconds, just to make sure they understood that I was mad, and that they were stupid!

I was a good way in front of them when I pulled off the highway and drove toward my home. Now it was really dark, the whole area too new to have working streetlights, and that's when I realized something: MY HEADLIGHTS WERE NOT ON! I hurriedly reached for the knob and could instantly see so much better. I could also see that the one I had called stupid was quickly coming up behind me at the stop sign, and I could tell that they were indeed following me. At each street, whether I turned right or left, they turned in tune and I knew that if I didn't shake them, I would be in for a confrontation.

Someone was mad at *me* this time, and I knew I had just enough road between us to pull into my driveway and quickly close the garage door. I would be OK, or at least in the safety of the house with brick and mortar standing between us. But then it would bring my husband into the fight, and he would learn of my foolish mistake of driving in the dark with my lights off.

I had raised the garage door in time, and I could have gotten out of the car and run into the house as it closed shut in her face, but I did not. I even surprised myself with what I did next. I waited in the locked car to see who I had wronged, and what their intentions toward me would be. A woman exited the car in front of my home, and I could tell she was full-on mad, and like I said, I surprised myself as I approached her, decidedly calm and apologetic.

I agreed with her that my mistake could have killed us both, and I offered her my sincerest apology, admitting that I had been in the wrong. I offered nothing in my defense, I WAS WRONG, and I told her so, and the change in her demeanor was immediate.

She had not followed me home to beat me up, though she was definitely MAD ENOUGH to, and how dare I be the one to indignantly hold my hand on the horn and aim anger towards her. She was enraged and wanted to express herself, and now that I had given her a platform, well, she just didn't need to anymore. My agreeing with everything she said had stopped her in her tracks, and I learned it is hard to argue with someone who is totally agreeing with you.

In the end we actually parted ways with a civil tone of caring for each other's future well-being. I had made a stupid mistake, and it could have been a costly one, but we were OK, no one had died. And she left feeling satisfied, because she had been 'heard.' We actually waved goodbye, as I watched her pull away before turning to the car to gather what was retrievable from the dinner sacks. I went into the house, feeling really good about the new way I had learned to handle a bad situation. I had allowed this woman her due and realized that the world could be a better place if we could learn to drop our defenses and truly own our mistakes.

A Stranger Connection

As my mother's health declined, I walked the path towards the inevitable with her. I spent several weeks at the hospital at her side, a foam pad in the window seat serving as my bed. There were times that I just needed a break, and while she napped I would walk through the parking lot to the nearby Costco for a slice of pizza.

It was July, and the air was warm. The sunlight gave me needed strength. I felt very connected to the Other Side, feeling my mother was close to crossing over to it.

The store was very busy that afternoon; it was the fourth of July holiday weekend. Holding my slice, I searched for an open table but found none. I opted for an empty chair at the table of a woman near my age. She welcomed my company, and it was nice to have some chit-chatty conversation that didn't involve the hard, life-and-death decisions I had been making on a daily basis. We spoke of jobs, husbands, children and grandchildren, before the conversation came around to the hospital. I was probably wearing my concerns on my sleeve, or how could she have known just how much I needed to talk. But she said that 'somehow,' she just knew.

I have said many times before that there are no accidents. An opportunity had presented itself to connect here in a noisy food court, and I opened myself up to her. We came to the subject of NDE's (near death experiences) and she said that she shared a fascination with the concept, but that she didn't understand why all the accounts she had read were so different from one another.

She was a teacher by trade, and I thought for a moment of the best, and most concise way to explain what I understood about it. An analogy came to mind, a book I thought she might be familiar with, called the 'Five Blind Chinese Brothers,' and I gave her a brief version of its valuable lesson:

> *There were five brothers standing around an elephant. Unfortunately all were blind, each touching a different piece of the animal, trying to describe something they were unfamiliar with.*
>
> *One stood behind it, taking a hold of its tail and remarking that the animal must be very skinny because his tail was so thin and rope-like, but the brother touching the elephants trunk disagreed, saying "no, that's not right," and that his tail was very large and malleable, while another stood at its hind leg and said "no, it was heavy and thick like the trunk of a tree." The one at the ear was describing something soft and flexible, like a leaf.*

You get the drift here, all of the brothers were right, based on the limited information they had in front of them. Each perspective was very different, and each was sure they had a very good idea of what the animal looked like. Of course, they would never be able to agree based only on what they had personally experienced.

She loved the analogy, promising that she was going to order the book for her class, because she could see many ways this could be used as an example and lesson. Wow! It was fun to feel like I had been a teacher too.

At the end of our time together, she expressed her joy in our visit, as did I in return. As she stood to leave, I told her to enjoy her precious granddaughter, adding that the way she had explained her, she sounded like a real 'itty-bitty,' and this statement made her stop in her tracks. She looked directly at me saying "how could you have possibly known that?" and added that the whole family calls her by a loving nick name of 'itty-bitty-gritty'. I had no real answer of where that added statement had come from, other than I just felt it, and with that we both chuckled and smiled as we parted ways.

Honestly, you just can't make this stuff up. When there is a connection, enjoy it, and bask in it, for there is a purpose in the connecting, and it will leave you both filled.

We had given a gift to each other that day, and it had been wrapped in a simple conversation, in a crowded and noisy room filled with perfect strangers.

Connecting
/kəˈnektiNG/ TO CONNECT
adjective

joining or linking things together, especially so as to provide access and communication.
"he went back to his office, leaving the connecting door open"

The Tree of Death and Life

Connecting with another person can happen anywhere, and today for me, a real exchange took place as I walked to my car. I was accompanied by the supermarket bag boy, and I could tell that this young man had plenty to say.

Earlier, the sales clerk had mentioned my necklace, a silver pendant replicating the 'tree of life.' I thanked her, saying I never took it off. Now moments later he was pushing my cart full of groceries, and we began a simple exchange about the weather and wind. But as I unlocked my car he told me he had also noticed the necklace because the 'tree of life' was very special to him, since 'the accident.'

I could have given a polite "thank you," and let the conversation drop as he finished hefting the bags into the back of my vehicle. But I allowed myself to be pulled in, and asked "What accident?" He seemed genuinely excited to answer my question. *"Did you hear the news story about the boy who hit a tree and died? Well, you're speaking to him."*

Now I hadn't heard of this particular accident, but he stopped to point down the street toward the tree that had changed his life. He spoke with a diminished capacity, clearly disabled, but he was speaking about my favorite subject, and I was truly interested.

I asked him what he remembered about his death, and if he had found himself in darkness or in light. And as he recalled the event, a beautiful smile crossed his face. He told me that he was surrounded in the most beautiful light, and that it was so bright that he could hardly see, but he knew that someone was beside him, and he was sure it had been his guide.

He spoke of The Divine Mother, and that he had actually talked with her and had learned why no one knows much about her, but since coming back, he was having trouble remembering.

We were in the middle of a fascinating exchange when it started to rain. We did not give in to the weather though, and we hunkered under the lift gate of my car to continue. He was so bubbly as he confessed that no one ever wanted to talk about what had happened to him or ask him anything about heaven. Apparently, I had been the first person who hadn't changed the subject when he tried to share his experience.

The wind suddenly changed and we began to get wet, but I felt I should stay put and hear him out. This sweet boy had a lot more story to tell, and he was hungry to tell it.

He was born to a mother who was in and out of rehabs his entire existence. He was addicted to meth from birth until he was five years old. He had known nothing but the street and its violence, having lost two of his friends to shootings from a gang in California. Shortly after relocating to Utah, he ran his car into a tree and died, and so far, that had been the best thing that had ever happened to him.

Our conversation ended when another bag boy came out to retrieve the shopping carts and told him they needed him inside. Before he left, he offered his name and told me to remember it and to look him up someday, because he was going to be a famous rapper.

He said his friends have told him to put his experiences into a book, but he said his story would never be found in a book because he didn't like books, and he didn't read books. And wasn't particularly interested that I was writing my second book.

He felt strongly that his message would be better served by being put to music. He was going to find a way to change Rap music, knowing that there could be better messages in the songs than what he heard at the time.

We both knew it was time for him to go back to work, but he turned around to face me one more time. With a boyish grin, he said he had always really liked trees, but now he liked them in a very different way. He felt a special affinity with trees, but especially with the one that had killed him.

I know I will probably see him again in the check-out lanes, but I doubt he will remember me. And that is OK, because I will never forget him or his story. He is the boy who ran into a tree and died, and then came back to life knowing that it was the best thing that ever happened to him. And I knew without a doubt, that he was already a part of the change he wanted to make in the world.

What a Difference a Few Kind Words Can Make

It is amazing what a few kind words can do. It can actually pump life into the veins with a literal feeling of being puffed up with renewed strength and energy. This gift came cloaked in a phone call from my Aunt Lajuana, a person dear to my heart, and one of the last remaining elders on my father's side of the family. Although I haven't seen her in years, her big smile and great laugh always come to mind when I think of her.

We had a wonderful visit, remembering old times and family get-togethers. We spoke of her memories of my dad, and how he knew how to tease her just enough to make her blush.

As we were neared the end of the call, she said she wanted me to know she had just finished reading my book. She said she had enjoyed it very much, finding herself laughing out loud in some stories, and crying at the end of others.

When I wrote my first book, I held an intention of being aware of the perspective of the reader. The material was carefully chosen from my journals, as I looked for entries that would open up thought, without offending anyone's religious beliefs.

I write of her 'review' now, not because of the compliments she gave me, but because of the deeper translation of its meaning for her. After telling me how much she liked it, her voice became lower and softer in volume, saying that in honesty, there were some parts that really made her pause and think. New ideas had been introduced that she had never considered before, and although she was 'still thinking,' many things had made a lot of sense to her.

We talked about the story of reincarnation and how the dream of my father had solidified my own belief that coming back again was more than just a possibility. She told me she was still in deep consideration of it, but because she had known me my entire life as a loving and caring person, and also because of the close relationship she had with my father, she 'TRUSTED' the information had come from a place of honesty and truth. She was sincere in thanking me for opening her up to some 'new ideas.'

She will never know how much her words meant to me, as they came from a place of love and trust. I now understand the phrase, 'feeling ten feet tall' after her kind words of reassurance. I write this second book with a renewed source of strength and conviction, adding writings of dreams that I still do not fully understand. But I write them with purpose, because I am supposed to. That is why I am receiving the dreams in the first place. It is because I am open to receiving and recording them with a sincere intent and to sharing them openly to be pondered.

Thank you Aunt Wonnie for the phone call, and for your honest confession of still pondering some of the unfamiliar information held within its pages. I can ask for no better compliment. It is a fulfillment of what I was meant to do in this life and it gave me the boost of confidence that I sincerely needed to proceed with the second book. ~ I Love You Always, Claudia

The Woman in the Babushka

We all have bad days, and it doesn't matter what constituted mine, but in recall, what comes to mind is the line from the movie 'Young Frankenstein,' when Eye'gore said, "It could be worse... it could be raining" and then the downpour began.

I can't remember if it was raining when I closed my eyes to sleep that night, but by the way I felt, it should have been pouring, and sometime in the night, I had one of 'those' memorable and teaching dreams, and although it's been several years now, I have never forgotten the feeling it left for me.

There was a woman in her fifties sitting on an old wooden bench, on an old cobblestone street, in an old town. I got the symbolism—this was from a long time ago. I took note of the way her heavy woolen wrap draped over her shoulders and layers of clothing. It made me think of Russia or Poland, and the words 'old country' and Bostrovia came to mind. Brown hair peeked out from under a scarf that I somehow knew was called a 'babushka,' a simple square of fabric, tied underneath the hair at the back of the neck.

She stood up when she saw me, and she stretched her arms out to me in a welcoming and heart-warming advance. I took a curious step towards the unfamiliar short and plumpish woman. I didn't know who she was, but I was drawn to her, just the same. My steps continued to erase the space between me and the woman who drew me near.

Her arms were so inviting, and she was holding them out for me alone, this magnificent stranger who apparently was no stranger at all. I felt a grandmother's love, the unconditional kind that a grandmother carries within her, and I was helpless in my need for it. It was real and tangible. I could feel it exude from her fingertips as she reached for me. All felt in slow motion as I moved toward her, and she mouthed the words, *I LOVVVE YOOUUU.*

She patted the seat on the bench next to her, and as I sat, she moved her hands up to my face and cradled it, and she brought her face to mine. As our foreheads connected I knew perfect love before I opened my eyes.

I lay in the residual feeling of what she left me, an elixir of the greatest power, and in its purest form. She had brought this healing medicine from across the greatest of divides, between Heaven and Earth, and apparently across several lifetimes too, though none was too far a distance to render aide to a loved one in need.

She was not my beloved grandmother of this lifetime, and I still wait for further recall of a life as her granddaughter in Poland, but I hold onto the undeniable connection I had with her, and the solid example of the forever connective strength of love and family.

All of the rest is secondary.
You are meant to help each other.

These words came to me early one morning as I woke, and I raced to my journal to capture them.

A life well lived is long enough

- Claudia Watts Edge

12

Life's Success Before Dying

"Personal measure and a time to accept and forgive"

Re-Friended

Six years ago, Brenda responded to a post I wrote about remembering dreams. She was a friend of a friend in the group, and she had clicked the 'like' button after reading one of my stories. At the time I was writing my first book about my nightly dreams of communicating with my angel sister from the Other Side, and about other miraculous experiences during my time as a volunteer hospice worker.

This is how Brenda and I began our friendship, spending several years exchanging 'likes, smiling emojis and floating hearts.' She was always so sweet to give me feedback on my writing and it was mostly positive, so it was a match made in Facebook heaven.

During the intensity of our government's elections, I could see by her posts that we did not share the same political views or candidate for that matter. I didn't think it was a big deal really, feeling that relationships should be valued, be it the linked in on-line kind, or the physical relations spilling blood over their different political views.

I noticed that I had not seen any posts from Brenda in a while, and upon investigation I found her missing from my 'friends' list. I had been un-friended. Too bad I thought, I liked her, and in spite of our political differences, we had many other things in common.

I thought of her from time to time, and when my book was completed, I knew that she probably would have liked a copy. But there was no way to contact her as I was blocked from her account, so I sadly gave up trying, and let her go.

It had been a couple of years since my unfriending, and I was genuinely surprised when I received a message from her. Her news was not good. She had been waging a personal battle against breast cancer, and she was losing.

The words showed up on my computer screen in short sentences. She typed from a chair, propped by pillows to keep her upright and breathing. This is how she lived and slept now, resting her hand that had swollen to the size of a bowling ball from the many steroid injections.

It took almost an hour for her to complete the letter, and I hung on every word that was slowly typed and sent my way. Over and over again, one or two words were typed before she pushed the send button. The sound of the alert became familiar, as the announcement of a new message went off over a hundred times. Eventually, the words formed a graphic description of the toll the surgeries and chemo treatments had taken on her.

She wanted to tell me she was sorry for the day she let all things political cloud her judgment. She admitted she had angrily cleared her account of all of us who held a different political belief than her own. Now as she looked squarely into the divide between this world and what comes next, there was clearly no time to waste considering which political side you were on. There were no more sides, only the grand abyss, and what is left to be done before you cross over it.

Brenda was determined to tidy up some loose strings, and apparently I was one of them.

I thanked her for contacting me. I told her there was nothing to forgive, and that I had continued to think of her as a friend and had always wished her well. She was crying as she said that it was me she had wanted to confide in when she was first diagnosed, and she had often wished she could call me as the cancer silently stole her strength.

Now as she faced the inevitable end, she wanted to talk to me about what to expect of hospice care. But most importantly, she asked if I would I share what I knew of the life beyond this one. She repeated several times that she was so sorry that she had cut the person out of her life that could have really been of help to her and her family in these last days. Forgiveness was easily given, and in the few remaining days before her death we arranged for a conference call with her family on speaker phone.

During the call I felt the ceiling lift away and felt assistance come over me as I calmly offered solace and words of comfort about an incredibly difficult topic. I gave honest answers about the dying process and what to expect for the patient and for the family who would be left to grieve.

We spent several hours hooked together in the miraculous technology that erased the 500 miles between us, repairing the quirky friendship of two people with many differences, but a need for each other just the same.

One can never really know the reasons why we are drawn to one another, perhaps this was the script and contract we agreed to long before we were ever born. Both of us played a brief but important role in each other's life play.

Brenda died two days later in a Denver hospice unit, but I will forever be thankful to have met and friended her, and for our foresight to make things right. We had an opportunity to say goodbye, and it was important.

I wanted to send her family a note, and I checked her Facebook status a few days later, but there had been no time or energy enough to re-friend me. I was still blocked from her account, and now it no longer mattered.

I am posting my best wishes for her here and will think of her fondly as she soars ever homeward, accompanied by many likes, pictures of angel wings, heart emojis, and smiley faces.

Karma Gettcha

On a busy Saturday, I ran out to do some errands just like everyone else in town. The line was long at the office supply store. There was a sale on shipping tape, and because we use a lot of it in our business, I filled my cart. I had a coupon declaring a $20.00 savings if I spent $50.00, but today there was an additional in-store coupon, which was great, but I would need to get a few more to get the great price. Not really an issue to get a few more, except there were four people in the line behind me, and there seemed to be only three working employees in the entire place. The clerk told me to go and get at least five more, and so I scampered three isles over to do a snag-and-grab in under 37 seconds.

I had to pass the customers in the line behind me to get back to the sales desk, and one lady took this opportunity to give me an exaggerated stare down as I passed her. She was probably my age, but her face had a chiseled meanness to it as she shook her head slowly from side to side with amplified disgust, as if I was the most thoughtless person in the whole world.

The clerk had not even finished ringing in all of the items in my cart, and my sanctioned dash to grab more did not extend the length of my purchase, but 'ole Crusty,' as I decided to call her, kept up her exaggerated stare down until her negative energy began to ripple through me with a laser's accuracy. It worked, and I was uncomfortable.

Another clerk finally called for the next in line, and she stepped up to the register behind me, but I could still feel hate flowing into my backside. She left me with an extra helping of snarl when she was finished with her purchase before all of mine was even bagged. Although I felt some relief that she had gone out the door in front of me, I was hesitant to follow her directly.

It wasn't that I was afraid of her, but she brought up memories of a time in my life that I would have retaliated, saying something ugly and snarling back. I am no longer interested in letting myself get hot while I swing my own negativity back, and believe me, I had can hold my own against any cursing sailor. But it all would have resulted in ruining my day, and I felt myself long past the need to jump into a lose-lose situation, by both my age and what I have learned spiritually.

I thanked the clerk for his help and proceeded out the door determined not to engage in her downspin, and I successfully got into my car for a clean get away. But she crossed my mind at my next stop just down the street at the grocery store. I thought, what if she was on the same path today and I ran into her again? Could I keep my cool? Have I learned not to engage but rather de-escalate a volatile situation?

I had no need to worry, she was not there, and I went about my day and filled my cart. At the check-out counter I was asked if I wanted help out to the car, "sure" I said, and the young clerk pushed the heavy cart out towards the parking lot when a rogue can suddenly escaped to the middle of the road, rolling away as we both chased after it.

It was comical really. This can with a mind of its own was causing quite a scene as both of us abandoned the cart to chase it down. It had lasted the briefest of moments, but when we stepped back to the cart, I turned to the car that was made to stop for us… need I explain the absolute perfection of timing and synchronicity because as you might guess, it was good ole' Crusty sitting behind the windshield of the car.

I couldn't help but to laugh out loud at the folly of it all, and I took it further by mouthing "Hi Crusty!" towards her in a pronounced and overly confident way, even adding a quick wave for sport. For whatever reason, this woman was meant to be bugged by me today, and I seemed to be doing a good job of it, while putting both of our demeanors on display.

I was able to witness the power of instant Karma, and her lesson of impatience and intolerance, but then I thought of my own behavior as I was enjoying this chance encounter just a little too much. I decided that I had better quit my celebratory laughing and move along, before my own Karmic lesson had time to arrive.

As my husband often says, "I don't care who you are, that's fuckin' funny."

The Cancer Holidays

There is no good time to be told you have cancer, but the middle of November seems poor timing, because like most everyone else, I love the celebration and joy the holidays bring.

Last year was a hard one for me. I had been ill for months with an unrelenting pain in my abdomen, and my days were filled with appointments for blood tests, X Rays, MRI's and CAT scans. A golfing buddy who was going through chemo for an aggressive cancer, shared a bit of sage advice with my husband, saying, "You don't have to start worrying until the doctors are the ones calling you."

One morning I got a call from an oncology doctor, saying he had been referred to my case and that he was concerned about my test results. The news was not good. I asked for his honest opinion and he shared that all pointed to pancreatic cancer. He wanted to see me as soon as possible, and was scheduling a PET scan, designed to look for any 'fast growing' cells within my body, and I remember giving a stunned yes to coming in ASAP.

The nurse was on the line before I had a chance to hang up. She had already been in touch with the hospital, but this is the time of year everyone is using up their remaining insurance benefits, and it was impossible to get me in anywhere until after the first of the year.

I would have almost seven weeks to ponder the possibilities and probabilities of what was ahead for me. I hung up the phone and reflected on the hospice patients I had cared for in my years of volunteer service and palliative care. Of all the cancers, pancreatic was not a good choice, and I reflected on the patients that had been brought down by this relentless and painful foe. The talented Patrick Swayze came to mind, having spent several years in a formidable battle with it, and he was eventually forced to surrender. It slowly gnaws at your strengths, eating at you from the inside out. It is unforgiving and fiercely painful, and I wondered if I had that same kind of fight within me.

My husband came home soon after the call. He said I had a 'funny' look on my face and I told him that I had just had 'that' phone call. I had never seen my husband cry, and I was a bit taken back by his instantaneous show of emotion. We both believed I was quite possibly facing a rocky road ahead.

The holidays approached and we would both stay busy putting up a good face in front of the family. We would keep this news to ourselves, determined to enjoy our gathering together as normal as possible before a complete diagnosis could be confirmed. We waited for January, and the start of a new year, though it was hard to hold back bouts of tears when alone.

I enjoyed every moment with my children, working very hard to make memorable gifts. Not a word was said, though everyone knew something was not quite right.

I include the only writing I was able to accomplish during this time, and I do so in the hope of promoting an understanding of a friend or loved one going through both the physical and mental anguish of disease and its uncertainties.

Halt, Who Goes There, Friend or Foe?

There are fewer and fewer days that I am successful at pushing, pushing down or pushing away an intruder that has taken up residence in my abdomen.

It grows more familiar every day, this act of pushing, and it takes up most of the space in my mind, my brain having to work overtime to stay useful within the perpetual fog.

This strange pain eats away at me from the inside out, taking on a life of its own, while taking away mine. It has become a loud companion who screams for attention, chipping away at the very essence of who I am, or who I was before losing the joy of being me.

There are hours in the day that it will wane and tire itself out, curling into a warm corner to rest, and I take advantage of this time like a busy mother while a cranky child takes a nap.

I am using this time right now to consider a different angle, adding a perspective from the pain's point of view.

The pain has a job to do. It's telling me that something is amiss, and something is not running properly in the machine that houses my soul. The yellow engine light is on, indicating a need to be serviced.

There is a commotion rising inside of me. I have listened to its droning and whining and I have parked myself in the mechanic's bay for servicing. I have found an excellent technician who sits directly in front of me, taking my hand, while looking directly into my eyes when he speaks. I am filled with hope as the softness in his voice offers me strength. We will work together to find the part, or the gear that needs oil.

Perhaps this pain is not my enemy, but a teacher who stands at the front of my desk, demanding that I wake up and pay attention. I have decided to be a good student and finish my homework, and then maybe the yelling will stop.

The Christmas of 2018 was made sweeter by the ache in my heart, and by the realization that this may be my last one. I guess this kind of news does help one appreciate life, holding onto both the sour and the sweet of it.

The Water Story

There was uncertainty about including this story, but after being compelled to share my cancer diagnosis, it seemed only fitting that I share the 'rest' of the story.

I woke one morning knowing what the news from my doctor would be. It would be good news, and I was going to be OK, and there was to be a reprieve of my health issues.

I had been in Spirit School, and there had been a lot of discussion of a new directive.

I was to receive more time here as Claudia, to complete a NEW mission. I sincerely enjoy my life, my children and my grandbabies, but I have accomplished what I had originally been born to do, my mission had been completed, and when the mission is accomplished, the soul yearns to return home like a tired soldier. I knew that my soul was looking for the exit sign, but apparently it has agreed to an additional assignment, and I have been allowed some extra credit duties before I go.

When in Spirit school, I always ask if I can bring something back with me, a precious memory of the teachings that I am allowed to share. I woke knowing that I had brought something back once again, but this time it was in a type of physical form. I'll explain.

There is need here on Earth, and I was given specific instructions of who and what the need is and what my ability to 'help' would be, though this has all been veiled from my memory now.

But... I was allowed to carry something back as an aide, I will call it Heaven Water, and I would be allowed to bring some back with me.

It had already been prepared, and a table held many large cups topped with plastic lids 'to-go,' the kind you would find at any fast food joint, and the irony of this was not lost on me. Heaven has a sense of humor, and laughter assists the memory. My guide uses this strategy, wearing outrageous costumes to get my attention in dreams.

I wanted to bring back as much of this 'help' as I could, and I began stacking these cups full of Heaven water in my arms. I was eager to collect as much as I could possibly carry, building a tower of them against my chest. Four on top of one another, and another topping the stack, for a count of five to-go cups full of the wonder of Heaven Water.

My arms were wrapped around this pyramid, the last cup resting against my face. Needless to say, my humanness was showing, and I took too much at once while trying to balance the impossible. My tower toppled over almost immediately. Three of the unbalanced cups fell to the floor, and the plastic tops popped off and spilled the precious contents everywhere.

"I'm sorry, I'm so sorry" I cried out, embarrassed by my greed, but there was only a generous chuckle from my guide "Don't worry about that" he said, "There will always be more available to you when you need it." And with that I was gone, but not home, and not yet awake.

I was still in a lucid dream state and standing in an unfamiliar dining room. Everything was old looking, and I viewed it like a kid forced to visit an old maiden aunt. A wooden table came into view now, covered with an old-fashioned tablecloth that held a dozen sickly looking plants, and under each pot lay a hand crocheted doily.

They could hardly be called plants anymore, most were no more than a woody stalk or vine with droopy brown leaves, as if they were thirsty and had not seen the sun in a very long time. I knew that these plants were the reason I held these cups of Healing Heaven Water. I was made to know that these plants were only a representation, of *'people'* who were my new assignment, and I heard the words, "*Help Them*" as I woke up.

In years past I would have worried what it was that I could to do to help. I would have spent a lot of time pondering what the metaphor of 'Heaven Water' really meant. But I have learned that there is much beyond our ability to 'see,' and I am content that I will eventually know who and what to do, when the time is right.

I have honestly not given it much thought until today, as I write this story after going through my journals. It is the story that was shown to be the last one included in the book. As I type it here, a blanket of knowing has covered me, giving me safety within its softness, and in this security came the word, "Knowledge."

I thought first of college, of the importance of education, and our continued need to learn. But as this thought came to me, a deep emotion was released, and I cannot stop my tears. I know that I had been guided to write down my dream journal entries for this very reason. I share them as I am doing now, and in doing so, I am offering knowledge to those who earnestly seek, and also to those who have withered in darkness like the woody stalks of the neglected plants.

If you are reading these words, please know that they are meant for you dearest seeker. Let yourself read with an opened mind and heart, accepting only what feels right for you. Examine it, pray about it, and hold it up to the light, the light of God/Source/and our Creator, and let its warmth and sunlight pour in.

Letting go of needless things

*Aging is the beautiful process
of letting needless things go
leaving more room for your own arms
to wrap around and hug yourself*

- Claudia Watts Edge

13

Aging is a Beautiful Process

A Jar Full of Minutes

I have acquired a sincere appreciation
for valuable minutes strung together
and the strength I have developed within myself
to claim them.

Perhaps a gift of growing old
a promise
to do with them as I please
If minutes were stored in a jar
I would reach in and grab them by the handful
never to be squandered

Why does it take so long to learn of a moment's value
when there are so few of them left?

- Claudia Watts Edge

Authenticity and Wrinkled Skin

My husband asked me a question this morning about aging and the neck. Actually, he was asking about HIS neck, now showing the signs of age. As realtors, we were getting ready for a busy day of showing homes, and as I curled and prepped, the television played an episode of Oprah Winfrey's 'Super Soul Sunday' and an interesting interview of Alanis Morissette. She was once a mega music influencer, who has now traded singing about the 'jagged little pill,' for a calmer gentler voice of identity and true self. As soul searching words echoed through our bedroom, I noticed my husband lean in close, and take a good hard look in the mirror.

Years ago, I found myself struggling to let go of an image of myself. I was clinging to a young dark-haired beauty who dieted and exercised incessantly. She ran in local 5 and 10 K races, wearing only finely tailored clothing from Nordstrom's and the like.

For a long time, my outward persona was a girl who enjoyed turning heads. But over the years, as hair dying, calorie counting, and flesh tightening undergarments became more needful, I noticed the stick I carried to beat back age was becoming heavier to wield. Was my life over now, as I found myself looking for comfort in the forbidden aisles of the elastic waistband?

My much younger husband has now picked up the torch, looking in the mirror at the silver frosting that is claiming the deep dark strands of his hair, and he asks himself, who is this person that looks back now? And what is happening to my neck!

It is hard not to laugh just a little, as he stares into the inevitable signs of aging. I saw a glimmer of hope as he remembered an infomercial about using some kind of tape to pull back the excess skin, thus achieving the flawless perfection of the youthful face we both remember.

Is it wrong to pursue our youth? Not at all. Some do it with gusto, injecting rejuvenated blood cells back into veins, or bovine botulism into deepening crevices. I have witnessed the culture of wearing a perma-surprise on Hollywood faces, the skin is so tightly stretched, that after the third facelift, the eyelids have a hard time blinking or fully closing. Maybe that's the answer, if you can't shut your eyes, maybe old age can't sneak up on you.

But sadly, it does, it sneaks up in a whisper, in the darkness, and in the soft ticking of the clock. When one decides to accept it is a matter of personal taste, the strength of the will, and the depth of the pocketbook.

I have watched my husband work very hard for the last two months, counting his calories and making extra trips to the gym, even though I still see him as the handsome man I married some twenty-seven years ago. We are both proud of the twenty pounds he has lost. He looks good, and I think he has stilled the hands of time, or at least wrestled them back a bit.

Hum mm, OK, maybe I'll give it another shot as I bend over to pick up the old age stick. I will hold it firmly against the forces that be, and perhaps I will I peruse the internet for some used exercise equipment that can be set up in the basement.

Time will tell... but then doesn't it always.

Tick Tock

I have read that time is an illusion and not relevant on the 'Other Side' but in the here and now as I live in this body, I am observant of it, perhaps even somewhat enslaved by it.

There are sluggish never-ending days, and the entrapment of the perpetual Wednesday-ness. I find myself asking a looming question of, "Why doesn't Sunday last longer?" Days come to a close, as do weeks and years, and as this body enters into the later of them, I am aware of my ever-slowing pace.

I am a grandmother now, and I am packing for a visit of my three-year old grandson Jude. I am to catch an early morning plane, but I have not yet set the alarm clock. I'm too tired to climb out of my sleepy state, and so I ask the universe for help to wake me up at five. Sure enough, for whatever reason I woke at 5:00 straight up, but I quickly rolled over for that precious 'extra' minute. And then I heard a cheery voice in my head saying "Dickery Doc." It came complete with a background beat of 'TIC... TIC... TIC... TIC... TIC... . This jovial announcement was as plain as day, and I giggled in fascination and wonder at the connection, and its response to my plea.

I spent four wonderful days as best friend to my grandson, feeling myself as happy as a five-year-old again at play. The morning I was to return home, I heard him softly chanting in the bathtub TICK TOCK, TIC TOCK and I understood his subconscious message. As time flees past us, we can only hold onto the NOW.

At the front door, he reached out for me in tears as we said our goodbyes. He pleaded for another day to spend together, both of us wanting more of this illusion we call TIME, and knowing that there is just never enough of it.

14

The Children Are Our Future

Speak to Your Children

*Speak to your Children
as if they are the Wisest,
Kindest, most Beautiful,
and Magical Humans on Earth,
for what they Believe
is what they will Become.*

For my littles with the big bold hearts ~ Love, Grandma Edge

Andrew Clayton Loecher, Ava Anderson and Zoe Anderson, Jude Clayton,

Addison Clayton and Sawyer Clayton, Jaydan Coulson and Harper Coulson,

Violet Gaskins and Churchill Gaskins, Joey Medina, Jessica, Marcos, Vanessa and Ryan Deherrera. With many thanks for their amazing parents, my children, who share their wonder with me.

Perfect Days

There is a large window above the sink in my kitchen that enables me to look out to my backyard oasis. As I do my daily chores, the stone pathway beckons me to follow it to the comfortable chair that sits under the flowering fruit trees. "Come and appreciate this perfect day."

But today is really not one of those perfect weather days. Although spring has inched ever closer, there is still a chill in the air as the snow is replaced by rain. I look from my window beyond the constraints of my yard and into the grounds of the neighborhood elementary school.

There were many who thought I might have a problem with the school being so close when I purchased this house. They said the children would be noisy and bothersome. But it is the sound of cheerful squeals as they run and jump, that holds my attention at this window every morning.

It is early, and the school day ahead has not yet begun. I can see the backpacks and book bags lined up in an orderly row against the wall that leads inside. The day is grey and the air is filled with tiny droplets of rain. It is just wet enough to keep many of us indoors, but not the children, and I let myself venture into reading the body language of their play.

The children are all so different in their looks, actions and sizes, and like every one of us, each one has their own story. They are you and I so many years ago when the energy within us was as bountiful as the days ahead. Ahh, to remember the days when the body moved before the mind, when running was easy and walking was for grown-ups and teachers.

There are only a few children who hold back from the school yard; it is raining and they stay close to the wall for shelter, playing in their own world as they squat next to their lunch boxes.

Others thrive in groups, their arms swinging wildly as they talk. They are expressive in their play, perhaps re-enacting a movie or superhero story, and they are engaged with one another in a common role.

Many practice acrobatic skills on the playground, vying for attention as others stand nearby watching and waiting for their turn to climb the hanging bars and polish their own skills.

I can see the limits of the grounds, and the fencing that safely corals them while keeping all others out. A few boys are hanging at these outer limits, alone together in a role of their own making, talking, trading cards or perhaps considering some mischief.

I think back to my own childhood days and try to picture myself within this busy mix.

Where would I place myself on this living canvas?

This is a group of individuals already practicing who they will be as they grow into loners, groupers, stoners, or doers and world changers. It is an identity that is not entirely set in stone, but it is definitely the early makings of who their adult selves will be.

The bell rings and there is a commotion of readying for the day ahead, and an orderly row is being formed. It is a practiced single file system and the wall hangers are the first to stand and take the important front spots in line. It made me giggle, thinking that they are the future hall monitors and politicians.

The playground acrobats scurry to their places behind them, while the ones furthest out keep a defiant gate in their walk. They use a system of calculated steps that is not quite a run, that will deliver them at the door just in time. They maintain an ultra-cool exterior, entering at their own pace at the back of the pack by choice.

I think of the adults these little ones will become one day in the not so distant future.

Another generation grows towards ruling the world, and I watch them in appreciation of the trials they will face as they grow. The hurts and pains, the loves lost and won, the achievements that might become part of the decor in their rooms. Or will they wallow in missed opportunities and the failings of their parents?

I thought of myself as a parent. Did I do my best for the children I brought into this world? Did I tell them they were special, capable, extraordinary, smart and talented enough?

Did I tell them they were awesome and did I show them that I loved them beyond measure?

I pray for the parents of these children, hoping they will not fall into a regret of their own failings, because there will be failings.

Life is hard, and there is just never enough... never enough money, never enough love, and never enough time.

We hear that time is really irrelevant, and yet we are living within its constraints. The sun rises and sets and there is so much to do in between. Soon enough we are looking towards our own personal winters, trying to capture and hold onto the rises we have left.

I watch the children as I let my own memories wash over me. I was a child once, who grew to bear my own children, and now they have children of their own. The world continues to spin under the warmth of the sun, giving life and solid ground to play and learn and grow. The sounds of the children are carried with the breeze into my window, and it offers a unique reminder: May I never take for granted the opportunity of living, even if it is while standing in front of my garden window.

Grandma, I Have Some Good News and Some Bad News

In the middle of a busy day, I got a phone call from my eight-year-old grandson Jude.

He began by explaining the details of a special field trip his class of second graders would be taking in two weeks.

Carefully choosing his words, he conveyed the details of a trip to Texas Roadhouse where the class would learn the art of making fresh cinnamon and honey butter rolls. The fun would continue with a performance by the students of another school. The day would be jam packed with activities and Jude had volunteered me as one of the helpers on the bus.

He told me that he had given it a great deal of thought and that he felt I was the perfect one for the job. He buttered me up, so to speak, as he told me not to expect a biscuit of my own at the restaurant, but that he would save a piece of his to share with me, if only I would come.

The sweet pleading in his voice, and a chance to spend time with him made it an offer I could not refuse.

The following weeks were very busy, including a business trip out of state, which left me tired. But I made a promise, and no amount of exhaustion would stand in the way of keeping my word. I would go and supervise a busload of children all day long and would find some kind of energy to perform these duties willingly. I would wear a happy smile that would make my grandson proud.

In the late afternoon the day before the field trip, the phone rang, and a teary voice held the other line, "Grandma," he said, I've got some news... and I heard a tear-filled sniffle and a big gulp of air before he continued "I've got some bad news."

Now I have received some bad news in my days, and I found myself in a familiar preparation for receiving it. I held my breath and gripped the edge of the countertop, before I thought, "Wait a minute, what bad news would this little man be delivering to me? And I relaxed my grip a little before I spoke. "What's the matter honey? Why are you crying?" My question gave him an opening to let out his frustration, and the tears in his voice were replaced by a defiant tone as he fired off a rapid line of mad filled words without a breath:

> "They are making me call you, they said they have enough
> Moms to come with us, and since you are a grandma, they
> told me they don't need you to come now, and I knew it

would hurt your feelings, and I don't think it's right, because first they said yes, and now they say no. It's not fair to you or to me!"

His tears began to fall again, and my heart melted at the love this little boy shows me. He has his own understanding of what is fair and right, and wrong in the world. His world, our world, and the difference in our perspective of it.

I had been tired anyway, and now I had been let off the hook without becoming a disappointment to anyone. But he had showed his true hero self, first in choosing his grandmother for assistance and companionship on his very important day, and now as a protector of my feelings. He is my true hero.

I told him I would be alright and not to worry, and that he should go on the field trip with his class and have a fun time. A compromise was made as we decided on a movie date on the following Tuesday, and we ended the call as his tears subsided.

As I hung up the phone, I thought of the perceptions we carry, his fear of hurting my feelings by having to ask me not to come, and my elation of getting to stay home without disappointing him.

We love and protect each other in our own way, and in many different ways. Sometimes the interpretation of love can be misconstrued and misinterpreted by our actions. And so I decided that after the movie, we should go to Texas Roadhouse for some hot cinnamon and honey butter rolls, so that he can teach me how they are made on our own terms.

Some Special Attention

Early this morning I took a walk in the rain. My destination was my son Aaron's home, because it is filled with three of my precious grandchildren, Jude, Addie and baby Sawyer.

The walk is not far from where I live, but it's an uphill trek, and the happy faces behind the front door are my reward.

Jude is the oldest, and he continually amazes me as he develops into a thoughtful and respectful nine-year-old. As I stood in the entryway for hugs, he took one look at me and raised his index finger, indicating to wait for a moment.

I continued my hellos but soon found Jude standing next to me again, holding a bottle of cold water in his hands, "Grandma I think you need this," and I paused, considering the many times he has been at my side in our midnight moon walks together. We wait for summer's long days to fade into darkness, and we watch for our moon to rise. We call nine or ten o'clock 'midnight,' as we gather our jackets and flashlights. It is a special time we share as we walk together, and we talk about everything and nothing, and all of it is important.

"Why thank you honey," I said as I cracked the cap on the bottle and took a long swallow. He added "I just knew you were thirsty" and he was right. I was thirsty, and I marvel at how well he knows me. He reads my face and the sounds of my breath as we walk and play, and he has recognized that I am beginning to slow down a bit.

One day as we chased each other under the playground equipment, he defended me in front of his friends by saying "My grandma's kind of slow, but she is really nice" and I couldn't have asked for a sweeter introduction.

Thanks for noticing me Jude and caring for me and for being even more than my beautiful grandson; we call each other friend and I hope that will never change.

Accentuate the Positive

In going through my journals, I came across a day spent with my grandson Jude. He had turned seven the previous week, and I find his young wisdom astounding. He is so easy to talk to, and has such an inquisitive mind, and generally weighs his answers with a beautiful integrity.

He had snooped in my desk while I was in the kitchen, and had told me so, mostly because he found a magnifying glass and was dying to explore its possibilities. After a talk about respect and privacy and the need to ask first, we invented a game of spy, and I left him clues in torn up pieces of paper for him to find. He spent hours crawling around the house looking through the glass for the secrets leading to treasures.

After he had discovered all of the mysteries I had hidden, we sifted through his loot. He made out pretty good, finding a roll of sweet tarts, some chocolate mints, seven pennies, and a sparkling blue crystal that I couldn't wait until Christmas to give him.

We decided to take a walk and explore the trees getting ready for winter. They were donning beautiful colors of yellows, oranges and reds, and we carried shopping bags to collect samples of each one. We spent hours looking for the perfect specimen from each tree based on its size and depth of color. This sample would be examined later that evening with the spy glass.

As we walked, the clouds began to roll in, and we would laugh and poke at the single drop of rain that would find our lips or eyes. Feeling the evening chill, I started to lament the end of summer and the great fun we had together at the community pool. I said, "It feels like summer is over honey, tomorrow will be the first day of fall, and it's going to get cold."

He thought about my statement for a moment before he added "Yes Grandma, but then we can always look forward to Halloween and jackets and blankets." I had to laugh while I hugged this little man who just can't help but find positive in the situation. Good lesson for me, Jude.

Epilogue

Small Bites

My near-death experience left me with more questions than answers, but also with a hard resolve to find the reason why so much of my experience was initially withheld from me.

I did find the answers, but they came in a slow and meaningful drip system, with a side of careful hand-holding lessons.

I asked my guide for the assurance that my reasoning was correct: that the withholding had been calculated and purposeful to draw out my own curiosity. Was I accurate in the assumption that my progression was tendered and portioned out in gradual doses?

I was literally following the breadcrumbs offered, and like a tiny bird, I was afraid to trust my own good fortune. My head would move from side to side in a fearful preservation of my own skin before taking a quick sample. I would look back again to check if anyone was watching before repeating the action again just a few steps down the trail.

But I kept following the path as it was presented to me, and each piece that I swallowed made me stronger, and I learned to trust. Now the tiny bird can fly high and with confidence.

And so, when I posed the question of WHY? to my guide, he answered me with his own question. Partly because he thinks he's funny, but also exhibiting infinite wisdom when he asked me,

"WHAT DID IT PROMPT?"

I am filled with gratitude for the small pieces I have been given over the years, because it would have been impossible to have carried back so much at once from my death experience. My answer to his question is contained in the stories I capture in my precious dream journals, and it has PROMPTED me to write two books filled with a need to share all that I have learned, all from this once fearful tiny bird.

I would offer, do not despair if you feel yourself at a crossroad in your own questions, as the answers will come in their own time. They may be offered in bits and pieces, in dreams and whispers, but be assured that the answers will come if you keep asking.

~ Claudia Watts Edge

For My Forever Sister

Our start was from the same branch of a substantial family tree
We were small shoots of green wood
Both pliable and vulnerable in our development
And we found our place in the sun to grow
The summers were shared between us
Ample in warmth and nourishment
The winters gave us pause as we shivered together in wait
I know you, my sister branch
And you know me, too
For all of our days shared together
And with the need for each other in common wealth
Our strength is bound together
In one another
My sister and I
And our growing family tree

Dear Mom

    This is the first time that Mother's Day will be celebrated since you passed, and I write this as I reflect back to the 62 years you were my Mom, in every sense of the word, Mother.

    I was always aware of your love for me, and I sincerely hope you always knew of my love for you, then, now and always.

I give Thanks for our 'Special Time' together in the hospital, the sillies we shared, even knowing the end was drawing near. We even joked of what that end day would be, you ever worrying about everyone else, not wanting to 'inconvenience' anyone with their summer vacations and birthdays etc. The date was not yet present on the headstone you shared with Dad for 45 years, your birth date ever present... but not an end date. Spiritually knowing there is no end, truly, but there is a time and date that brings a finale to our being able to go see a movie and dinner together, or to sneak off to Iceberg for a malted. I will miss the physical fun times we gave to each other... now to be remembered.

We did a good job of respecting and loving one another. I will not dwell on opportunities we may have missed, or things we didn't get done. Rather, I will reflect on a warm day we sat in an indoor/outdoor café in New Orleans. It was a trip picked by a blindfold, a map and a stickpin. We were adventurous, you and I and Kaylyn, trying drinks of chicory, and doing our best impressions of remaining lady-like as we licked our fingers while eating 'beignets,' a fried dough delight coated in white confectioners' sugar. We laughed and pointed at each of our faces covered in sticky sweet powder from nose to chin.

We had so much fun at our hotel slumber party. Our giggles came easily, at times holding a pillow over our face as not to disturb other guests.

I am grateful for the ease felt in each other's company, and I miss your company now. It has been almost a year without a phone call and a "what'cha doing, hahaha." The sound of your laugh will be forever missed.

I hold onto the dreams I have had of you since your passing, and I am grateful for them. They are the gift of the 'one more time,' or the 'one more day' we plead for after our loved one passes. There is comfort given me from the dreams of you and I doing normal worldly stuff. I 'SEE' you, and you look great; you are smiling and happy and that gives me encouragement to carry on, that you are near me always, in love, in memory, in thought and dreams. I know you are close and I speak to you often, and sometimes when something happens that is our kind of funny—well I can almost hear your laugh again.

So, Mom, I will close this letter to you by saying Happy Mother's Day Mom, with an appreciation of you and the sacrifices you made on my behalf, and for your patience with me as I stumbled, and then held back in patient anticipation as I found my way.

I am at peace knowing that when I feel alone, all I need to do is hold out my hand, and that you are taking a hold of it in kind, in support, in pride and in a love that a mother freely gives, and this is how I will remember you always.

I Love You for all of time Mom,

Your Daughter Claudia

I wrote this letter as I sat in an outside garden coffee shop, with an empty legal pad staring up at me. I didn't feel like working, the day was beautiful, the sky a pale blue and the slightest breeze moved the clouds above me. I thought of the times my mother and I shared moments like these together. I missed her; she was my best friend, and it had been less than a year since she passed. I wrote this letter, hoping that she could see it, and could hear the words as I wrote them.

That evening as I slept and dreamed, there was an 'interruption' in the regular sand dreams of nothingness, and I became lucid and awake within the dream. I noticed a picture of my mother, but it was upside down, and as I picked it up to fix it, I realized that I was holding an answer from her, the upside-down picture was a representation that although things were different now, she was still there with me, and gave a complete confirmation that she knew of my letter.

I have included the letter to her here, as a sincere thank you and acknowledgement for the lessons she has given me, many as a Dear Mother and her child, and many from the Other Side, still involved in my continued development.

Thank You

"Someone once said that a writer and a spider are to be pitied above all others because they both are left hanging by a thread spun out of their own guts." Thank you Charlene Daniels for sending me this, and other reminders of your faith in me, and your decades of friendship and support. You are the one who got me into this crazy business of baring my heart and soul on paper.

To Deirdre Dewitt Maltby whom I knew in my deepest depths that I was meant to find you. To Joan Edge Pearson for your early editing and always safe place to fall and be filled. To my constant companion Click Click who is always there in full costume, for the grandest effect, and who patiently waits for the opportunity to teach me another valuable lesson.

Thank you to the many, you know who you are, who offer feedback of my stories and continued support when I grow weary. You nudged me into writing again by asking me "when is the next book coming?" before I had even considered writing it. This question was valued, and honestly meant so very much to me.

Shout outs to Ellen Dye and Rod H McCallum Jr. and Lajuana Watts, for lending me your beautiful words.

To Greg Unterberger, Dr. Rohit Gour, Becki Hawkins, Mary Deioma, and Charol Messenger, thank you for your kind reviews, and foreword, and for your understanding of the birthing process and the intensity of bringing a new book into the world. Your words offer encouragement that it is not an ugly baby.

Thank You to the talented Curtis Pearson for another beautiful cover.

A very special Thank You to John Melody for being an answer to my prayers and rescuing this book in its final stages of completion. You are the kindest of souls, and a valued friend.

Thank you to my brother Jeff Watts, who surprised me by reading every word of my first book and gave me a treasured hug while saying "keep on writing sis," there is a special star in heaven with your name on it Jeff, I saw it.

To my son Jesse Clayton, thank you for allowing me to share such personal accounts of our lives together, and for spending endless hours on the phone as we explore the spiritual mysteries.

Much gratitude to all of my beautiful Children Sarah, Jesse, Aaron, Eric Ricky and Chelsea Rose and Grandchildren who make my life worthwhile, and to my always and forever Chris Edge for all he does for us.

Thank you to my special muse with the dearest heart, Jude Clayton, for our inspiring discussions of the whys and why nots of EVERYTHING.

A special heartfelt thanks to my Angel Sister Kaylyn, my mother Lillian, and my Dad, Bud Watts for the continued contact through the veil, and for the teachings they share with me in my dreams. Until I see you again...

About the Author

This is the second book for award-winning author Claudia Watts Edge. The first book of the series GIFTS FROM THE EDGE was 'Stories of the Other Side.' Claudia has always shared her life events through storytelling, feeling it an important form of communication. She lived in Colorado Springs for many years and worked there as a real estate agent and hospice volunteer. She is currently living in Salt Lake City Utah with her husband Chris and enjoys public speaking and sharing the wonders of the spiritual connection with IANDS (near-death experience) groups. She loves spending as much time as she can with her children and grandchildren, who are a consistent source of inspiration for life lessons and insight.

In love and light,
Claudia Watts Edge

Made in United States
North Haven, CT
16 November 2022